Assessment of Student Achievement

Assessment is a concept familiar across the field of education and is inherent to the work of professors, administrators, teachers, researchers, journalists, and scholars. A multifaceted and politically charged topic, assessment ranges from informal interactions with learners in classrooms to systematic high-stakes testing and examination. Written by a leading expert on assessment, this book situates the topic within the broader context of educational psychology research and theory and brings it to a wider audience. With chapters on the fundamentals of assessment, explanations of its uses, and advice for best application, this concise volume is designed for any education course that includes assessment in the curriculum. It will be indispensable for student researchers and both pre- and in-service teachers alike.

Gavin T. L. Brown is Professor and Director of the Quantitative Data Analysis and Research Unit in the Faculty of Education and Social Work at the University of Auckland, New Zealand.

Ed Psych Insights
Series Editor: Patricia A. Alexander

Assessment of Student Achievement
Gavin T. L. Brown

Self-Efficacy and Future Goals in Education
Barbara A. Greene

Self-Regulation in Education
Jeffrey A. Greene

Strategic Processing in Education
Daniel L. Dinsmore

Cognition in Education
Matthew T. McCrudden and Danielle S. McNamara

Emotions at School
Reinhard Pekrun, Krista R. Muis, Anne C. Frenzel, and Thomas Goetz

Teacher Expectations in Education
Christine Rubie-Davies

Classroom Discussions in Education
Edited by P. Karen Murphy

GAVIN T. L. BROWN

Assessment of Student Achievement

Routledge
Taylor & Francis Group
NEW YORK AND LONDON

First published 2018
by Routledge
711 Third Avenue, New York, NY 10017

and by Routledge
2 Park Square, Milton Park, Abingdon, Oxon, OX14 4RN

Routledge is an imprint of the Taylor & Francis Group, an informa business

© 2018 Taylor & Francis

The right of Gavin T. L. Brown to be identified as author of this work has been asserted by him in accordance with sections 77 and 78 of the Copyright, Designs and Patents Act 1988.

All rights reserved. No part of this book may be reprinted or reproduced or utilised in any form or by any electronic, mechanical, or other means, now known or hereafter invented, including photocopying and recording, or in any information storage or retrieval system, without permission in writing from the publishers.

Trademark notice: Product or corporate names may be trademarks or registered trademarks, and are used only for identification and explanation without intent to infringe.

Library of Congress Cataloging-in-Publication Data
A catalog record for this book has been requested

ISBN: 978-1-138-06184-2 (hbk)
ISBN: 978-1-138-06186-6 (pbk)
ISBN: 978-1-315-16205-8 (ebk)

Typeset in Joanna MT
by Apex CoVantage, LLC

Contents

One: **Purposes and Functions of Assessment**   1

Two: **Embedding Assessment Within Curriculum, Teaching, and Learning**   13

Three: **Classroom Assessment—Teacher Judgement**   29

Four: **Involving Students in Assessment**   57

Five: **Feedback, Grading, and Reporting**   73

Six: **Objectively Scored Assessments**   87

Seven: **Scores and Statistics**   109

Glossary   126
References   135
Index   150

One
Purposes and Functions of Assessment

'Educational assessment' refers to the set of methods and processes by which evidence about student learning is designed, collected, scored, analysed, and interpreted. These processes are meant to support decisions about teaching (e.g., What material needs to be taught again or differently?), learning (e.g., What material does a student need to revise?), administration (e.g., What students are ready for promotion to the next grade?), policymaking (e.g., What areas of the curriculum need teacher development?), and accountability (e.g., Which schools add more value? or, Which student should be given the supreme scholarship prize?). The processes depend on expert judgment and statistical analysis of the quality of the assessment methods, their relationship to intended objective or outcomes, and the validity of consequences.

However, everyone already 'knows' what the purposes and functions of assessment are because of their own assessment careers (i.e., a person's experiences throughout life related to being tested, examined, or evaluated[1]). People have had various experiences of being assessed in school, sports, artistic endeavours, clubs, and at home. Take a moment to reflect on your last assessment experience. What happened with the assessment? Here are some possible consequences, some educational and others not so much.

2 Purposes and Functions of Assessment

- Was it reported to your parents?
- Was it filed and forgotten?
- Was it used to put you or someone else in a different learning group?
- Did the teacher go back over some topics?
- Did you get a grade or score?
- Were you told how well you were doing compared with other people just like you?
- Were you held back a year or term because you didn't do as well as someone thought you should?
- Was it sprung on you with no warning?
- Was it marked fairly?
- If you did well, were you told what you had to learn next?
- If you did poorly, did the teacher ever suggest that maybe the test wasn't quite up to scratch or that the teaching was the problem?
- Did you go home with a happy smile, knowing that you would be rewarded for your A or 97%?
- Did the teacher announce—with concern, scorn, or pride—your score to the class?
- Was the assessment even marked?

Based on the multiple and diverse experiences learners have with assessment across their lives (i.e., assessment career), their personal beliefs concerning the purposes and functions of assessment begins to form. The research literature variously calls these beliefs 'conceptions' or 'perceptions' of assessment.[2] The goal of this chapter is to formalise the multiple purposes and functions of assessment so that an educational approach to assessment can be taken. The goal of this volume is to help readers develop a conception of assessment that is focused on using assessment to improve the quality of teaching and the quality of learning.

I consider that why and how we use assessment (not the form or type of assessment) is what really matters in assessment, and so how assessment is conceived matters. If assessment is conceived as oppressive, students who gain greater understanding of assessment theory will not necessarily believe that assessment improves their life chances (a situation documented in a case study of New York teachers in a masters level assessment course[3]). This approach is consistent with theories of reasoned or planned behaviour that state that an individual's beliefs, which are influenced by peers (i.e., social norm), relate to intentions and practices.[4] Thus, a conception of assessment is highly likely to shape anyone's uses of assessment.

PURPOSES OF ASSESSMENT

Newton[5] describes 17 different purposes for assessment and others provide different functions, though attempts have been made to simplify the list by aggregating the functions into meaningful groups.[2] I organise my thinking about assessment around three fundamental questions:

1. Is assessment useful?
2. If it is useful, when does assessment take place in the educational process?
3. Independent of timing, is assessment aimed at informing improvements in the processes or at evaluating the quality of the processes?

The first question raises the possibility that assessment is fundamentally pointless, irrelevant, and possibly even bad.[6] The second question raises the importance of timing: Is it done early enough to lead to some useful change or is it done at

Purposes and Functions of Assessment

the end, when nothing further can be done? The third question points to two fundamental goals of assessment; that is, improvement versus accountability. Together these questions lead to nuanced opinions such as:

- Assessment X didn't seem to do anything except keep us occupied.
- Based on my scores on Assessment Y, I was refused entry into Advanced Placement (AP) Chemistry.
- Assessment Z told me exactly what I needed to work on so as to improve my performance.

Conceptions of assessment are tied to specific events and processes, but over time people are likely to form an overall opinion about assessment in general. These conceptions include:[2]

1. Assessment provides useful, accurate information so that appropriate changes can be made by teachers and/or students to raise the quality of teaching and learning (improvement).
2. Assessment shows whether schools and teachers are doing a good job in ensuring students can do and understand what society expects (school accountability).
3. Assessment shows whether students are achieving what is expected of them, judges the quality of their performance, and awards grades or certificates accordingly (student accountability).
4. Assessment is so flawed, inaccurate, and inappropriate that we would should ignore it (irrelevance).

Here's a hypothetical example of some teachers talking[7] about assessment. What conceptions can you identify embedded in these opinions?

Purposes and Functions of Assessment

Five teachers (A—E) stand at the notice board in a school staff room and read a new notice: 'Ministry of Education releases new assessment tool for literacy and numeracy. Contact the Regional Office for your copy.'

A: See! All they're interested in is checking up on us. How can they keep using tests to decide if we're good teachers or not? What's the union doing to protect us?

B: Nah, tests are just a way to make the rich, white families feel good about paying heaps for the extra fees that their schools can charge. Our kids haven't got a hope of doing well. It's just part of a plot to keep minority students down.

C: That might be, but you know what to do, don't you? If they make you use it, just do it, write the scores down and forget about it and carry on doing what you always do. After all we're good teachers; we know what our kids are like and what they need. We don't need any tests to help us do a good job!

D: I'm not so sure about that. I've seen the trial stuff when our kids did it last year. The kids in my class really enjoyed them—it made them work a little harder and feel good about themselves. I think this kind of assessment might just motivate our kids.

E: Well, I've seen them too, and I think the reports will help us do our jobs better. There are all kinds of descriptive information in them about what achievement objectives kids need to work on, what their strengths are, and what they've already mastered. It gives you all sorts of good ideas about where to start and who needs what.

Conceptions Exercise—Discuss With a Partner

1. Which teachers expressed views of assessment as improvement?

2. Which identified assessment as a means of making schools and teachers accountable?
3. Which saw assessment as a way of making students accountable?
4. Which thought assessment was irrelevant?

You'll find my answers at the end of the chapter.

FACTORS IMPINGING ON CONCEPTIONS OF ASSESSMENT

It seems logical that, as circumstances change, educational participants (students, parents, teachers, policymakers) form different emphases in their conceptions of assessment. For example, New Zealand has a strong policy of using assessment to improve student learning, so formal tests are used at the school level to inform educational practice.[8] Unsurprisingly, teachers strongly believe that this is the purpose of assessment and feedback.[9,10] The New Zealand practice is to identify student learning needs through systematic analysis of assessment data and attempt to diagnose the causes and monitor the effectiveness of changes.[11] In contrast, formal testing of students at the end of the year is used extensively in the United States and the United Kingdom to determine whether students and schools have been doing a good enough job.[12] Indeed, students are held back a year for low grades, school leaders are dismissed for having low grades, and ranks are published, resulting in kudos and/or shame. In such circumstances, teachers may rationally develop a conception that school accountability testing is not just irrelevant but also wrong and consequently act to subvert the system (witness the 2015 case of teachers jailed in Atlanta, Georgia, for cheating on student tests).

Purposes and Functions of Assessment 7

Because assessment is connected to curriculum, teaching, and learning processes, conceptions of assessment are influenced by how those processes are viewed. Additionally, how you conceive of assessment is strongly influenced by the norms of the cultural or social group you belong to. For example, teacher-centred direct transmission of knowledge and effortful learning by students are coupled with high respect for teachers and formal examination in East Asian societies.[13] Hence, assessment (especially testing) acts as a legitimate means of motivating students, rewarding diligence, and overcoming negative social effects such as promotion through collusion, corruption, or nepotism. Teachers in such contexts tend to view assessment as a legitimate means for improving student learning and character.[14] Kennedy[15] argues that, despite nominally being associated with Confucian approaches to learning, these social norms more properly are a consequence of high-pressure, low-opportunity public examination systems seen in East Asia and in many other developing world contexts.

Becoming aware of how a person understands and relates to assessment matters since their conceptions filter and guide their interpretation and implementation of assessment.[16] This matters considerably for educators who have to implement policies imposed by management or government. If teachers have to do the work but don't share enthusiasm for the policy, then it is difficult to believe they will do it as intended (remember the 2015 Atlanta teacher case). It is clear that teachers are squeezed between two major functions of assessment that both have legitimacy.[17,18] The first, most strongly endorsed by almost all studies of teacher conceptions of assessment, is assessment that informs teachers as to who needs to be taught what next, which is commonly called 'formative assessment'. The second, often rejected by teachers but frequently endorsed by parents, is assessment that identifies the quality of schools, teachers, and learners and holds them to account for their performance, which is commonly referred to as 'summative assessment'. The legitimacy of these competing functions arises in the first instance from the simple assumption that the role of teachers is to help students improve, while in the second instance those who fund teaching have a right and need to know if they are getting what they paid for. Hence, teachers are in an invidious position in which they will be judged for how well students do on tests which at the same time ought to reveal needs that, by implication, the teacher has failed to address—a classic position between a rock and hard place.

STUDENT CONCEPTIONS OF ASSESSMENT

However, many readers of this volume are likely to be students rather than teachers. From that perspective, what are the legitimate uses of assessment? Unsurprisingly, students are conscious that at one level assessment is meant to inform them as to their learning successes and identify their learning needs. Ideally, assessments also motivate and guide students as to what they can do to overcome any needs they have. Students are well aware that assessment is used evaluatively to determine whether they should be given passes, scholarships, qualifications, or certifications, and to assign them to extra tuition or remedial education, if scores merit such. Studies of New Zealand high school student conceptions of assessment have shown that greater endorsement of both improvement and evaluation functions of assessment is associated with greater achievement.[19,20] Assessment also has an impact on student effort,[21] emotions,[22] and motivation,[23] and it triggers dishonesty.[24] How students prepare for

Purposes and Functions of Assessment

assessment, and react during and afterward, all contribute to greater or lesser outcomes.[25] Being assessed is stressful, in part, because of the uncertainty of not knowing whether (a) personal expectations will be met, (b) enough preparation has been conducted, (c) the assessment will sample the material the learner has studied, (d) the assessment will be too hard, (e) the marking will be fair, (f) the learner is 'smart' enough, (g) the student's family will be happy with the results, and so on. Classroom assessment takes place in a social space—students tend to have a sense of where they stand relative to others. An individual's capacities are not invisible to classmates since they can be seen in group projects, public performances (e.g., speeches, reports to the class), or displayed on the classroom wall. This means assessment can bring out the best or worst depending on the individual's psychological stance toward making weaknesses visible to others.

Hence, it matters that students have adaptive conceptions of assessment, such as: (a) assessment informs me as to what I have mastered and need to work on, (b) my teacher will help me by teaching me the things I did not succeed on, (c) I need do my best because it is my learning, not the teacher or the school, that is being judged, (d) facing up to hard and challenging tasks and questions helps me improve, (e) being anxious is understandable but it should not stop me from trying, (f) I will learn more by keeping to the honour code, (g) my results do not depend on my ability, but on my effort, and (h) my classmates can help me improve and I them. It seems quite clear that how you conceive of assessment contributes to your results; constructive conceptions lead to greater self-regulation of learning and greater learning outcomes.

There are a number of questionnaires that will help an individual become more aware of their own thinking. For example, my *Student Conceptions of Assessment* inventory[26] provides insights as to how strongly four major purposes of assessment (i.e., improvement, external attribution, classroom climate and emotions, and irrelevance) are agreed with. Go to https://doi.org/10.17608/k6.auckland.4596820.v1 for a copy of the questionnaire. For each statement indicate the degree to which you agree or disagree. Note that the response scale is not balanced—there are more shades of positive because I think most people are inclined to agree with these statements. Respond to these statements based on your own experiences and opinions; don't try to guess what you 'ought to' say. There is no 'correct' answer—respond based on what you really believe, even if it isn't what you've been told to believe.

CONCLUSION

So what does all this tell us and mean for people involved in education? First of all, how individuals already conceive of assessment impacts how they will interpret and put into practice the lessons of this book. If teachers constantly think assessment is about grading students' innate and fixed amount of ability or intelligence, or that it is a function of teachers' personal prejudices, then it will be difficult for them to use assessment results to critically examine what parts of their teaching need to be changed. Alternatively, if teachers think assessment is about grading, classifying, ranking, or measuring students, then it is likely they will assume that poor scores result from weaknesses in the student rather than in their teaching. However, this book will try to demonstrate that low scores may be a function of poor assessment practices; for example, the assessment may not be aligned to the teaching, items may be poorly written, assessments may have been administered unfairly, the scoring may have been too subjective, the meaning of the student performances may have been interpreted poorly, or the reporting to parents or students was inaccurate or unhelpful.

I consider that professionalism in assessment first considers the possibility that assessment practices were to blame for poor results before deciding that something else is to blame. And further, if the assessment was done suitably, instead of blaming students (e.g., they did not study enough) or society (e.g., the students have poor parents and so cannot learn well enough), I consider that the professional teacher should consider that the teacher's own teaching may need to be changed. But before a teacher can be open to the possibility that assessment is about informing their own teaching practice, the teacher must have a belief that the purpose of assessment is not accountability of students or schools, but rather improvement. Thus, before teaching you about assessment, it is important to consider pre-existing opinions gained through experience about the purposes and nature of assessment.

It is important to remember that not everyone has exactly the same conception of assessment, even though there are strong similarities among people in similar environments. This is an important consideration for school leaders or policymakers who wish to introduce changes. Failure to use assessment to improve school or classroom practices may come about because the leader has different conceptions of assessment than the teachers working in the school. Failure to analyse school assessment data may indicate lack of assessment skill or it may indicate that teachers believe that such action is not what assessment is for. Students who fail to use assessment to improve their performance may have any number of ancillary beliefs and practices that hinder their improvement, or, more simply, the assessment may provide so little information (e.g., total score or rank order only) that improvement is not feasible.

In the next chapter, I will introduce the principles of assessment that are essential for effective and appropriate education to take place. There are many ways to approach the more technical aspects of assessment (i.e., the strengths and weaknesses of techniques). Rather than beginning with multiple choice question writing and formal methods of testing and examination, I propose addressing the heart of classroom assessment—that is, the teacher who judges quality and the students who comment on and evaluate their own and their classmates' work. Within this context, I will include feedback and reporting as communication arising from essentially human judgements. Then, I will approach the more classic techniques of objectively scoreable testing, both digital and paper-based. I will introduce some of the many standardised test scores (e.g., percentile, stanine, etc.) while drawing attention to their strengths and weaknesses. The volume will then conclude with a reflection on what we know about assessment.

Answers to Conceptions of Assessment Exercise for Chapter 1

Here is my take on the teachers' conceptions revealed in the conversation earlier in the chapter:

1. Assessment is related to improvement of student learning and teachers' teaching (teachers D and E).
2. Assessment evaluates the quality of schools and teachers (Teacher A).
3. Assessment certifies that students have learned or met standards (Teacher B).
4. Assessment is irrelevant to the work of teachers (Teacher C).

Two

Embedding Assessment Within Curriculum, Teaching, and Learning

Students of education need to know how experts understand assessment. Simply put, assessment is the process of making appropriate interpretations and taking appropriate actions based on appropriate collection of information about valued content.[27] The focus is not on a method or technique; rather the focus is on how assessment information is interpreted and what is done with it. The actions resulting from assessment determine whether an assessment was fair, appropriate, and valid.

Assessment has powerful social consequences for all involved. No one wants to fly from Washington to New York with a pilot who has been only 50% successful in landing a Boeing 737 aircraft on the flight simulator, let alone in real life—the consequence of getting it wrong is too high. Indeed, we would all love to know that our pilot has the skills of Capt. Sullenberger, who safely landed his unpowered jet on the Hudson River with no loss of life. If assessment is done badly or poorly, the consequences might not be as extreme as crash-landing with a poor pilot. Nonetheless, most readers can probably recall a teacher whose assessment of their work was invalid, leading perhaps to false perceptions of potential and capabilities. Professionalism requires that instructors know how to assess well so that assessment contributes to an accurate understanding of and appropriate responses to student performance. The risks of disaster may be much lower in schooling than in medicine or aviation, but low quality in assessment processes can and does have an impact on the child and their family.

Society expects, and most curriculum frameworks require, that the learning of children is monitored. Assessment must be done well so as to fulfil that requirement. This places assessment at the heart of education: curriculum, learning, and teaching intersect in assessment. Assessment requires strong, theoretically well-grounded knowledge of learning materials and sequences (curriculum), instructional actions (teaching), and what it means for students to 'know' something (learning).

PRINCIPLE 1: CURRICULUM ALIGNMENT

Good assessment begins with a curriculum which specifies what students are expected to learn, understand, or make progress in (e.g., know the names of the planets of the solar system, appreciate similarities in the two world wars of the 20th century, be able to type 35 words per minute with no more than 5% errors). It is absolutely critical that these learning objectives, goals, or intentions are valuable.[28] While trivial things (e.g., the middle name of the current president) are easy to assess, they are rarely what schooling aims to teach. Curricular statements generally specify at what stage of learning (e.g., Grade 4, Key Stage 2, Level 2, etc.) various skills or knowledge are expected and provide standards of performance expected for each skill—these define the content (i.e., skill or knowledge) for assessment. In addition to content expectations in learning areas (i.e., subjects or disciplines), curricula tend to also specify the kinds of cognitive processes students need to engage in (e.g., analysis, synthesis, abstraction, recall, etc.). A number of useful taxonomies exist, but it is generally accepted that society expects children to think deeply, use higher-order thinking skills, and process complex material in systematic and rigorous ways. While the ability to remember or recall is necessary, assessments that do not require deeper thinking will fail the curriculum and society. Alignment of the assessment to the curriculum, also, ensures that the content of an assessment is coherent with a learning area and matches what has been or will be taught in a classroom. This ensures that an assessment moves from being a type of general intelligence test to being a guide to classroom instruction and learning.

PRINCIPLE 2: EXPLICIT CRITERIA AND STANDARDS

Good assessment specifies—derived from the curriculum—what successful performance looks like. In other words, if we want students to 'understand the solar system', we need to specify in advance exactly what we mean by *understand* (e.g., Do we mean to make sense of or just recall some material in the textbook?) and what we mean by the *solar system* (e.g., the names of the planets, the process by which the solar system was formed, the sizes and material make-up of each planet, and so on). Further, we need to specify standards by which we will determine whether a student's responses or actions indicate success: in other words, 'how many' or 'how much' or 'how well' are required to provide sufficient evidence of 'understanding the solar system'. Another way of understanding what explicit criteria are is to ask: What is the answer? What does the assessor expect the learner to know, understand, or be able to do to satisfy the requirements of the objective?

Clearly, appropriate standards have to fit such factors as the age of the learner, the nature and amount of instruction, and our societal expectations. What might be expected of a 10-year-old will be different to that of a university undergraduate, let alone of a university professor. Consider the graduated driver licencing scheme as an example of incremental standards. In New Zealand, a learner driver is someone who knows the rules of the road well enough (i.e., passed the learner knowledge test with 90% correct) that they can begin to learn to pilot a vehicle under supervision; a restricted licence indicates that the driver knows the rules and the skill of driving well enough (i.e., passed the practical learner driver test) to drive a vehicle solo; and a full licence says that the driver knows the rules and the skills of driving well enough (i.e., passed the practical full driver test) to carry passengers at any time of day or night unsupervised. The quality of driving skills seen in a learner is so basic that this is signalled to all other road users by having a large L sign displayed on the vehicle. Cars without such a sign are assumed to be driven by people who meet the standard for unescorted driving, giving us a level of confidence about how the vehicle in front, beside, or behind will behave.

Teachers might legitimately expect that a detailed specification of what is expected (i.e., skill, knowledge, or cognition and content) would be available in the curriculum. However, for many reasons, a curriculum document is usually not sufficiently specific to help a teacher decide if students have learned enough of one skill (e.g., addition) to be ready to be taught the next more difficult skill (e.g., multiplication). In such a case, a teacher must turn to other sources (e.g., previous experience, colleagues, professional associations, school policy and practice, etc.). Nevertheless, criteria and standards need to be clear if teachers are to design appropriate assessments. In the ebb and flow of classroom activities, the teacher may rely on an intuitive sense of what quality and progress look like; this is sometimes called 'assessment *as* learning'.

However, the more explicit these criteria and standards are, the more effective the teaching will be and the more credible assessment decisions will be. Knowledge about criteria and progressions is part of teachers' content knowledge—the teacher must know what mathematics at Grade X looks like in terms of content and difficulty in order to assess it. This is true for all learning areas at all levels.

Further, this content knowledge must be partnered with the teacher's pedagogical knowledge of how to teach that content. For example, knowing how to subtract negative numbers must be partnered with knowing how to teach subtraction of negative numbers. For assessment to be fair and just to all concerned and for reporting to be meaningful, the criteria and standards being used to judge the quality of student learning (whether for reporting or improvement purposes) need to be explicit to both the teacher and the learner. Indeed, this principle of transparency has been shown to contribute to improved learning outcomes.[29,30]

PRINCIPLE 3: METHODOLOGICAL ROBUSTNESS

Once we know what we want to assess, we need to select the best mechanism for collecting meaningful information about the learning targets. Scientific research in education requires the most direct method of data collection.[31] For example, if we want to know if a trainee hairdresser can cut curly hair well, we probably should not ask trainees to write an essay that asks: *Discuss similarities between curly and straight hair in the hairdresser's salon.* A straightforward performance of cutting three to six curly or straight heads of hair, combined with client satisfaction feedback, would probably satisfy such an expectation. The best way to assess the skill is to measure it directly. Hence, in many disciplines, the use of school-based, performance assessments of important curriculum objectives (e.g., ability to give a speech, perform in a drama, conduct an experiment, etc.) is the norm rather than reliance on paper-based testing. The fundamental principle is that the data-collection methods must be suited to the type of objective and type of learner.

A further consideration here is that every method of assessment has its strengths and weaknesses. For example, a multiple-choice test covers a lot of information efficiently and is reliably scored, but items are difficult to create and students select rather than demonstrate knowledge. In contrast, an essay test can cover the ability to integrate or synthesise information and forces students to compose their own version of knowledge, but is extremely difficult to mark consistently. Mixing types of assessment methods may create a more rounded appreciation of what the student has learned, though it needs to be asked whether performance is consistent across methods of data collection. Should we expect the ability to give a speech to be highly correlated with answering multiple choice questions about Lincoln's Gettysburg address? Teachers are expected to create and administer assessments of ephemeral events (e.g., speech-making) because society wants young people to learn to do things that are hard to capture. With the advent of low-cost audio-visual and computer technology, capturing ephemeral performances is relatively straightforward. However, ensuring that a robust, representative sample of performances has been obtained is challenging, as is the complexity of ensuring that marking, scoring, or judging is sufficiently robust.

PRINCIPLE 4: IMPROVEMENT-ORIENTATION

While assessment serves multiple purposes (see Chapter 1), the educational purpose for assessment is to identify who needs to be taught what next. Will the assessment be used to guide teaching or is it simply fulfilling an administrative requirement? While it is possible to conduct assessment just for administrative reasons, it is undesirable if assessment is done only to occupy or get control of learners. Torrance and Pryor[32] described in detail how teachers of young children in England could be seen to be using assessment to control the behaviour of their students. There is evidence that regular testing can motivate students to pay attention and improve, provided the tests tell teachers and learners what they need to know to improve.[33] However, weekly test results can also be ignored by teachers and become an irrelevant and possibly negative educational process.[34] Thus, unless assessment results are going to be used by the teacher or the student in a meaningful way, there may not be a valid educational reason to conduct the assessment.

Teachers can take a range of actions to improve outcomes, including (a) change what and how they are teaching, (b) change the group that a student is in, and (c) report to the student about their learning. Likewise, students can, among other things, use assessments to (a) identify their weaknesses, (b) applaud their successes, and (c) identify improvements they have made.

Figure 2.1 shows an ideal assessment cycle: the content that we want to teach is decided, teaching is implemented, assessments are designed, and interpretations about progress and needs are made. With these in hand, instructors and learners begin to plan what they should do next; teachers think about what they need to do with the curriculum and students, while students are expected to consider what changes they might make. Having made these updated plans, teachers begin a new round of curriculum planning and teaching of the valued content.

Embedding Assessment Within Curriculum

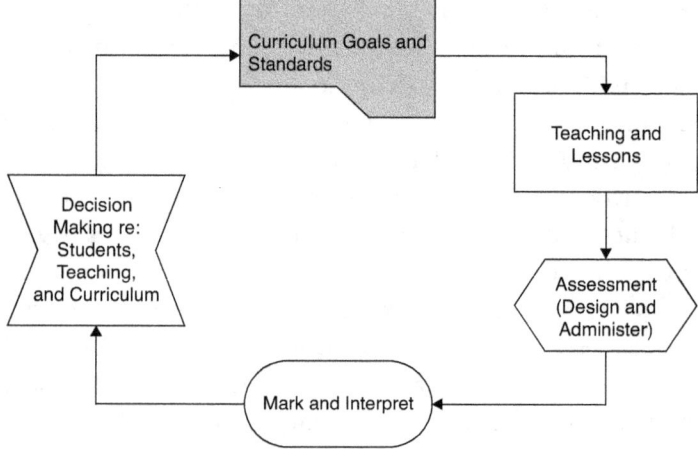

Figure 2.1 The Curriculum, Teaching, Learning, and Assessment Cycle

ASSUMPTIONS FOR ASSESSMENT METHODS

Having established the integral role of assessment in teaching and curriculum, it is apropos to consider some important constraints on what assessment can actually do. These issues speak to causes of low validity or low reliability in any assessment.

1. Assessment is always a sample of the skills, knowledge, and understanding a person has. A census of everything in a domain is not feasible. Hence, the sample used to guide interpretations and decisions is always flawed and imperfect. Good assessments create high-quality samples, but samples always have error in them. Hence, the question is, Have we got a robust enough sample of the right data on which to base a decision? Assessment is a set of inferential judgements based on a sample of behaviours. One technique for ensuring quality sampling is to ensure

sampling in multiple contexts (e.g., formal written tests, oral interactions in class, homework handed in, etc.).
2. The material that is easy to test is not necessarily the material that the curriculum values. Beware of valuing the easy-to-test, rather than assessing the important-to-learn. Hence, robust assessment requires planning and organisation by the teacher.
3. Testing, measurement, assessment, and evaluation are tightly interconnected.
   a. The terms can be distinguished along the following lines:
      - testing is the use of formal paper-and-pencil, objectively scored events;
      - measurement is the establishment of formally defined numeric scales using some statistical technique;
      - assessment is the determination of what students know and can do through any means, including tests, but predominantly through judgement-processes; and
      - evaluation is the determination of the value and worth of some product, process, or programme, usually done systematically and summatively.

   In contrast, the ERIC Thesaurus treats assessment as a type of evaluation. This means that there is no one way to use these terms. Generally, *assessment* is an omnibus term covering all types of data collection, including standardised testing and a teacher's professional judgement of how much and what a student has learned.

   b. The real difference between testing and assessment, if there is one, lies in the types of interpretations or actions that various processes can support. Formal, explicit assessment processes mean that public consequences can be introduced (e.g., it will be safe to fly with a captain who has done well in real-plane practice of take-off and landing). Teachers' informal interactions with students in a classroom may lead to insightfully correct interpretations of need and strength. Such anecdotal evidence may not provide a robust basis for formal reporting, but it may lead to important directions for corroborative assessment.

4. The teacher's role in assessment has changed. Traditionally, teachers taught, while central or external examination authorities assessed. Teachers needed only to mimic public examinations so that students were prepared for the official examination. In many Western countries, however, teachers are required to collect evidence and exercise interpretive judgement about learning as teacher-assessors. This means teachers have to become assessment literate or capable.[35] For teachers to be assessors, they must be considered by society as competent to collect, evaluate, and respond to evidence appropriately. Otherwise, students and parents—let alone administrators—might look askance at a teacher's professional classroom practices. Competence and capability in assessment comes from expertise in content knowledge, pedagogical content knowledge, and assessment literacy.

5. There are many questions around collecting information that need to be considered. For example:
   a. Which method is best able to elicit the performance in a fashion consistent with the desired or intended learning outcome itself?
   b. Should learners have time to prepare a product or should work be on demand under invigilation?
   c. Should the assessment be part of a portfolio collection over time or should the task be a one-off event, like an examination or test?
   d. Should the learners be allowed lots of or little time, and should resources be allowed or not?

The point here is that the methods of assessment used must be appropriate, sufficient, and trustworthy. They also need to be manageable.

6. Assessment generates information about what students can do and know. Students are aware of what they are being assessed on and can use that information, as well as later results, to guide their own learning. However, the teacher has responsibility for deciding what is taught, when it is taught, how it is taught, and how classroom learning is organised. Thus, assessment for teachers is about reflecting on what they have done and could do next. For a teacher, assessment ought to be primarily about what changes, if any, the teacher needs to make so as to more effectively teach each and every student according to their needs—in other words, to practice differential assessment.[36] Instead of focusing on whether students are clever or lazy, teachers need to focus on *who needs to be taught what next*. Assessment is how a teacher takes responsibility for instruction; the results tell the teacher what was learned and what was not, and they consequently inform the improvement of teaching.[34] Like the surveyor's theodolite, the engineer's calculator, and the carpenter's rule, assessment is a tool by which a teacher determines the effectiveness and direction of her or his own work. You may have heard that farmers do not help their animals grow by constantly weighing them, and therefore teachers should not constantly test their students. Nonetheless, good farmers monitor animal health, growth, and output to modify their farming practices. Hence, the argument I advocate is that, by careful consideration of what the various assessments tell the teacher about student needs, the teacher can craft a teaching programme that meets those needs. Assessments that provide only a percentage correct

or a rank-order score do not give teachers the kind of information they need to make appropriate changes. Diagnostic insights are needed from all assessments.

7. Despite the importance of teacher professionalism in assessment, students play an important role in determining whether teaching is effective. Assessment can be a very negative experience for students, especially when they feel powerless.[37,38] Students sometimes blame teachers or schools for poor results; others will do just enough to meet minimum requirements, rather than their best.[39] The point here is that the effectiveness of assessment depends, in part, on the active intelligent engagement of students.

8. Good-quality interpretations depend on good-quality assessment processes. While assessments with more questions tend to produce more reliable discriminations between more and less able participants, the cost of a long assessment (e.g., time lost from instruction, fatigue impacting effort or motivation) might mean that the assessment leads to lower-quality information. Consequently, good assessment design is a compromise around competing factors that can raise accuracy in scoring at the cost of reduced validity. The simplest way to express this assumption is the classic computing expression GIGO (garbage in, garbage out). Thus, all assessment processes (e.g., designing an assessment, administering and scoring it, interpreting its meaning, planning an appropriate response, and so on) need to be evaluated to determine whether each step has been done well. For example, if the assessment is worthwhile, but the instructions are unclear or ambiguous, then the validity of the assessment is questionable. If the assessments are inaccurate or

invalid anywhere in the process, then the interpretations will be misinformed.[40]

9. Assessment is fundamentally about determining the quality of learning; that is judgment-scoring. Quality can be inferred from a sum of correct answers, or from a holistic rating or judgement. Such qualities are frequently converted to a score or grade (e.g., percent correct, letter grade, normal curve equivalent, stanine, etc.) in the hope of more efficiently communicating important information. All such quality judgements capture the notion of progression: that is, somewhere between complete novice with little or wrong knowledge, skill, or ability, and expert with very high knowledge, skill, or ability. Just as road signs and distance markers help us assess how much of our journey we have completed and how much further we have to go, so assessment converts learning progress to a scale that enables easy communication and appropriate decision making. Nonetheless, even good progress scales can be misunderstood and can introduce error in our communication.

10. Every assessment process contains errors; even the metre is not a perfect measure.[41] While systematic sources of error can be identified and minimised through robust assessment processes, there will always be discrepancies between two or more types of assessment, two or more judges, and two or more times. This is even more noteworthy when we assess something as imprecise and fleeting as classroom learning. This does not mean formal or standardised testing is a doomed enterprise, rather it means we must instead be honest and humble about the potential for inaccuracy in our judgements and our assessments of children's learning.

11. As in all professions, teachers have ethical, let alone legal, obligations to show that their assessment practices have been fair, unbiased, and appropriate.[42–44] The consequences of assessment actions must be defensible and not lead to differential impact (i.e., proportions greater than 80% of the reference group) depending on construct-irrelevant factors such as ethnic group, sex, or socio-economic class.[45] It is the teacher's responsibility to ensure that a low score really is attributable to low skill, knowledge, or understanding, rather than to poor testing practice or biased scoring by the assessor.

THE PREPOSITIONS OF ASSESSMENT: *FOR*, *OF*, AND *AS* LEARNING

Much is made currently of the three prepositions of assessment—assessment *for*, *of*, and *as* learning. Assessments conducted *during* the learning process and at the *end* of the process are usually called 'formative' or 'assessment *for* learning' and 'summative' or 'assessment *of* learning' respectively. 'Assessment *as* learning' refers to assessment-like interactions (e.g., questioning) between teacher and learner during instruction. However, what students and teachers learn from the process of interaction assessment may not be what was intended by the lesson plan or curriculum—and this may or may not be a good thing. However, it is highly probable that the evidence obtained 'in-the-moment' or 'on-the-fly' will be an inadequate sample of student learning and will require follow-up structured assessment to ensure validity of subsequent interpretations and actions. It seems to me that intuitive judgements carried out on-the-fly in the classroom might be better understood as teaching rather than assessment.[46]

Embedding Assessment Within Curriculum

There is some considerable debate in the research literature about the relationship of formative and summative assessment, with strong implications that formative is good, while summative is bad. Indeed, Sadler[47] has argued that assessment during instruction is intrinsically different to assessment at the end of instruction. However, I subscribe to Scriven's[48] position that assessment during instruction must be of the same quality and standard as that conducted at the end. If the teacher is going to use the information to change teaching and really expects that change to improve the quality of learning, then the assessment information had better be as accurate and informative as it is possible to obtain. Hence, it seems better not to treat formative and summative as qualitatively different assessment practices but rather as different times, and thus uses, of assessment.

Some assessment for learning advocates[48,49] have argued that formative assessment is what happens for students (i.e., increase in their motivation or improvement in their learning) and that there is little place for educational tests or teachers. Clearly, as long as students are intelligent consumers of education, their motivated involvement is essential. However, formative assessment cannot exclude teachers, who are the responsible professionals in the classroom.[50,51] This is not a case of being teacher-centric; it is a matter of teachers taking responsibility for guiding student learning. As long as learners are not expert in the material they are learning, they require insights that the more-expert instructor can give them, and research shows that students want that input.[38,52] Hence, it is the responsibility of the teacher to effectively monitor learning progress so that appropriate instructional actions can be taken.

Although summative assessment is at the end, it is possible for summative assessments to be used by teachers and learners as information for the next round or class. Such use might not help the group of learners just finished, but it certainly can be and frequently is used to improve the quality of teaching for the next group of learners or the next topic. In other words, formative and summative are cyclical and mutually beneficial if we want them to be. We do not have to accept the old chestnut 'formative good, summative bad'.

SUMMARY

This chapter has overviewed educational assessment; that is, the use of assessment to improve educational processes and outcomes. Much of what we do in assessment is problematic; the possibility of error abounds. Professional teaching requires grasping this complex process, fully aware of what might go wrong, while tentatively exploring the meaning of each answer, product, or performance that students provide. The constant refrain needs to be, Who needs to be taught what next?—while bearing in mind that it may be what the teacher has done that needs to be changed.

Three
Classroom Assessment—Teacher Judgement

There are many important insights about student learning to be gained by collecting evidence that shows what students can do (i.e., what they can create or construct). Assessment has the potential to show us the depth and complexity of student understanding and skills. These processes are necessary because in most fields there is no one correct answer—only better or weaker responses. Thus, the teacher or marker has to make a judgement about the qualities of the work; that is, the work is judgment-scored. Unsurprisingly, this is not an exact science; it is rather more an art, but one hopefully that can be done in a high-quality fashion dependent on rigorous analysis of evidence.

THE RUBRIC

We need a robust framework for making sense of the educational products, processes, or performances that learners create. This framework has to do double duty: (a) guide teaching and learning as a progress map and (b) guide judgements about quality of work. A rubric (sometimes known as a marking scheme, progress indicator, progress map, or matrix) is a statement of characteristics associated with different levels, standards, or grades of performance by which the work can be understood. A rubric depends on a clear understanding of what the learning intention is and what the stages of progress towards that learning intention are. This is an expression of one of the fundamentals of measurement—describing the journey towards a desired result in terms of meaningful, learnable, or teachable units.

The process of using a rubric to guide the scoring of student work or processes is called 'rating'. Rating is the declaration of an assessor (usually an expert in the content or skill) that the work under consideration is best described by a certain category on the progress scale. What we need to understand, then, is how best to craft rubrics and how best to ascertain whether our ratings guided by a rubric are sufficiently trustworthy that we can base educational decisions on them.

There are many different labels for indicating degree of progress. For example:

- New Zealand high school qualifications use Not Achieved, Achieved, Merit, and Excellence.
- Hong Kong high school qualifications use grades E, D, C, B, A, A*, and A**.
- England uses Key Stages 1 to 4 in its primary and junior high schools.
- The United States' National Assessment of Education Progress at Grades 4, 8, and 12 uses Below Basic, Basic, Proficient, and Advanced.

In all these systems, each label is a short form for a potentially complex description of a certain quality or quantity of skill, knowledge, understanding, or ability. Professional judgement assessment, then, is the matching of the learning product, process, or performance to a labelled stage of progress towards the desired goal. A rubric, thus, is a progress scale, wherein the progress units are attached to descriptions of learning, and rating is assigning a progress unit to a piece of learning.

Designing a Rubric

Two major kinds of rubric exist: holistic and analytic. Holistic rubrics attempt to capture all important aspects or features of the work into an overall classification. For example, the terms and grades commonly used at university (i.e., Excellent = A, Good = B, Average = C, Poor = D, and Weak = E or F) usually express an assessor's overall rating of a piece of work, taking all things into account simultaneously. While there may be some variation within the work, the overall rating declares that the work fits best within a certain grade range, which itself contains variation. When a doctoral thesis is examined, the marker is asked to express their overall opinion in holistic terms—pass as is, pass with minor revisions, pass with major revisions, or resubmit after new work is done. The classification is a weighted judgement by the assessor taking all things into account at once; hence, it is holistic.

In contrast, analytic rubrics specify various dimensions or components that are evaluated separately and, hopefully, independently. The same rating scale labels may be used as in holistic rubrics, but they are applied to various key dimensions or aspects separately rather than as an integrated overall judgement. This separate specification means that on one dimension the work could be excellent, but on one or more other dimensions the work might be poor to average. Most commonly, analytic rubrics have been used by teachers to score student writing in which separate scores are awarded for (a) conventions or mechanics (i.e., spelling, punctuation, and grammar), (b) organisation, (c) content or ideas, and (d) style. They are also used in many other domains of the school curriculum (e.g., performing arts, sports and athletics, studio arts, wood and metal technologies, etc.). By breaking the whole into significant dimensions or components and rating them separately, it is expected that better information will be obtained by the teacher and the student about what needs to be worked on next.

To illustrate both types of rubric, consider your evaluation of a favourite food (chocolate chip cookies, potato chips, guacamole, etc.) for which there are multiple choices in the marketplace. Putting price aside, consumers select a food by aspects that are appealing in the taste, feel, smell, and appearance of the product. A holistic approach to any food simply places the product's overall impact on a scale that might range from 'so horrible I spat it out' to 'so delicious I can't stop at one or even two,' and there may be one or more intermediate stages between the end points. The point of a holistic rubric is that a decision can be made relatively easily as to whether more of a product should be bought, but little information is gained as to why the judgement was made. What aspects of the food caused the reaction? Unfortunately, such a rubric and rating provides little direct insight as to what changes, if any, need or can be made. Thus, in education, if holistic rubrics only are used, students would not know what they were being judged on, just what grade they got. This means holistic rubrics are best suited to situations where feedback or further learning is not expected; that is, in a summative end-of-course evaluation. Alternately, they might be useful when the rating has to be done extremely quickly, as in the scoring of Olympic diving or figure skating. The event being rated happens so quickly and there is so little time between performers that analysis of the scoring cannot be done, nor is the situation deemed to be 'educational' (i.e., an Olympic event is the final exam, not the formative preparation). This type of assessment is summative in its timing and is assessment of learning.

However, if the goal is formative and educational, more information about the various characteristics of the product is needed. A chef looking to create the perfect guacamole depends on tasting it regularly to make appropriate adjustments to various aspects of the dish (e.g., the colour, saltiness, citrus level, texture, etc.). This can be done intuitively, but when customers are asked to rate and comment on the new recipe, it will help to have an analytic scale which identifies key features of the dish that could be modified. In order to rate each key dimension of the dish, the developers have to describe the main dimensions that are to be evaluated and the scale categories that the raters are to use in describing each dimension. This provides a matrix (i.e., dimension by scale category) that guides the assessment and provides a basis for comparing judges. It is worth noting here that developing and using an analytic rubric requires considerable content knowledge so as to make the nuanced decisions needed to tease apart the various aspects of a piece of work. Furthermore, even if there are only three dimensions to rate, this approach requires three times as many decisions as a holistic rubric and, thus, considerably more work. This suggests that asking students to make judgements might be better using a holistic approach since they are unlikely to have the skill or time, especially in early stages of their learning, to fully utilise an analytic rubric. Clearly, an analytic rubric is aligned to assessment for learning or formative assessment in that the goal is to gain information as to how and where changes could be made.

The rubric is the basis of scoring essays, portfolios, performances, and other complex work, whether by the teacher/assessor or the students themselves. Assigning a descriptor to a learning object is not a precise science; it is a complex judgement of a competent expert. These judgements need to be validated, at a minimum, by comparison with another marker. It is always possible to get judgements wrong. Next, I present some techniques for reducing the error attributable to inconsistent human marking.

Moderation Within Rubric Use

The degree of precision, accuracy, and consistency or reliability in a set of scores can be estimated easily in a school context: (a) by comparing the degree to which the same essay is given exactly the same or approximately the same scores on separate times or by separate raters (consensus) or (b) by finding the degree to which the pattern of high and low scores is similar among markers or markings (consistency).[53] This requires that at least two different markers rate the work using the same rubric and then compare their scores. Reliable and trustworthy scoring can be defended when one or more standards are met:

- At least 70% of items receive exactly the same grade.
- At least 90% of items receive approximately $(+/-1)$ the same grade.
- The correlation between markers is at least $r = .70$.
- The chance-adjusted correlation kappa between markers is at least $\kappa = .40$.

In these circumstances, scores can be defensibly issued to administrators, students, and families as agreed upon by two or more competent markers.

However, when these standards are not met, a process of negotiation needs to take place to resolve the discrepancy. Normally, a pair of markers would debate only those items where the disagreement is substantial. Each marker would need to identify the characteristics of the work that merit the higher or lower mark awarded. Since two heads are better than one in many situations, gaining insights from a partner marker can lead to much-improved ratings. If the raters can persuade each other and reach a compromise, then the agreed mark or grade becomes the one that is used. In the event of severe disagreement between any pair of judges, some moderation schemes make use of a third judge (e.g., a chief examiner or head of department) who resolves the discrepancy, although the final agreement may simply depend on the original markers deferring to the authority of the third judge rather than actually agreeing that the score reflects the merit of the piece of work.

Improved agreement between markers depends on a number of factors. Markers need to be trained how to use a rubric, and regular check marking by another person is needed. Discussion as to differences in scores between marker and check-marker will help improve consistency among judges.[54] Nonetheless, even highly professional and controlled marking can result in acceptable but relatively low indices of reliability. For example, the College Board AP examinations reported in the 1990s that for four subjects (i.e., English language, European and US history, and Spanish literature) the inter-rater correlations fell in the range .76 to .78. This suggests that achieving high levels of agreement between raters is challenging.

THE EXEMPLAR

A powerful adjunct to a rubric is an exemplar, which is a product that has been selected to exemplify a certain point on the rating scale. Often the exemplar is a top-of-the-scale piece that represents the intended learning outcome well. Having an exemplar makes the rubric's descriptor language more realistic and accessible to students and teachers, and, importantly, reduces the marker's need to rely on memory of top performance when making judgments. A facet of a good exemplar is that it includes annotations identifying features of the exemplar and making explicit their relationship to the rubric. In the selection of exemplars, annotation should be incorporated to help future users (whether markers, teachers, or students) understand why and how an exemplar fulfils the requirements of the rubric rating category.

Permanent exemplars are straightforward when the learning object is on paper and can be easily disseminated online. When the learning object is ephemeral (e.g., a dramatic performance, dance, or speech), 3-D (e.g., a machine, sculpture), or digital (e.g., a web page or piece of code), then video, audio, or digital capture and preservation technologies are needed. An assessor can use a technology-based exemplar from any location, at any time, allowing more flexibility in the assessment process.

Exemplars are intended to improve the consistency of judgements between and among markers and to allow students a better understanding of what the rubric really means. Selecting and annotating exemplars both have a powerful effect on the people involved in those processes; however, once the rubric published and distributed, the challenge is to ensure that future users actually refer to it when carrying out assessments.

SOURCES OF ERROR IN HUMAN JUDGEMENTS

Research with human marking of essays and other performance assessments has established why and how mistakes are made in judging the quality of such work. Over the decades it has been generally established that human judgements tend to be inconsistent not only between judges but also within judges. For example, only with strong attention to ensuring consistency do ratings of essays reach the thresholds for reliability described earlier.[54–58] This might suggest that we shouldn't use humans at all to judge or rate or mark student work and instead rely on machine scoring. This is not a real option yet, since computer assessments of essays—let alone complex products like oral language or scientific reasoning—cannot readily assess the higher-order skills we value.[59] Identifying sources of error in human marking is useful because it will indicate things we can do to improve the quality and dependability of human marking.

Students

Differences in scores are expected among students; not everyone is at the same place in learning or has the same mixture of abilities or competencies. So assessment tasks are meant to detect differences in students' performance that reflect real-world variation in their abilities. Using generalisability theory methods, it is possible to determine that much of the variance in human scoring can be reliably attributed to differences in students themselves.[60] Nonetheless, students can be affected by random events or circumstances (e.g., home life problems) which can impact on their performances at the time of assessment. What this means is that circumstances irrelevant to their real abilities can negatively impact on performance.

While home life factors might be out of the control of schools and teachers, it is up to the teacher or assessor to ensure that the assessment context or environment has minimal distractions. The environment needs to be conducive to maximal student performance. Hence, heat, light, and noise levels in the room must be supportive of 100% effort. This might also mean that schools have to ensure pupils are first given breakfast and a chance to play outside before any assessments are conducted. It might mean avoiding certain time periods known for low-quality productivity (e.g., the old maxim that cars built on a Monday traditionally were of lowest quality).

Topics or Tasks

The quality of the actual task or prompt that directs the student has a moderate impact on performance.[61] Clarity, conciseness, and completely unambiguous instructions are needed to ensure that students are pointed in the desired direction. Topics must be realistic and achievable for the students being assessed while being sufficiently challenging and worthwhile. However, students have different prior knowledge, motivation, or attitude for different topics. Also, not all topics are equally difficult.

If teachers are trying to draw conclusions about student competence in a field, it is important to remember that completing a performance task requires significant time by the student, reducing their ability to collect multiple samples of the student's ability or knowledge. It may well be that student performance on Topic X is not a good predictor of a similar task on Topic Y (e.g., the ability to write a persuasive essay on global warming is not a predictor of the ability to write persuasively about the value of international travel). This is always a risk of a single sample. Analysis of performance tasks in high-stakes assessments in the United States has indicated that about nine tasks from one pupil rated by one rater were needed to achieve a generalisability coefficient in excess of .80[62] and that between seven and nine hours of testing time were needed in English literature and English language to attain generalisability coefficients of .90 or higher.[63] Thus, to reduce the effect of the one-time essay on the student, it is useful to take multiple samples of the same ability and to distribute those samples during the school year and week.

It is also clear that students respond differently to different topics, so accommodating personal preferences by offering multiple occasions with a variety of topics will give a better sense of student performance.[60] It needs to be clear here that the best way to offer choice is not by giving multiple prompts at one assessment and letting students pick whichever they prefer; rather students should address the same topic at Time 1 to ensure reliable judgments and be allowed to do other topics at later times.[61] Students, especially in primary or elementary school, should address many different topics over the course of a school year to ensure that their observed performance is not handicapped or advantaged by a certain topic. Brennan[60] has shown that students should be given at least three essay tasks before a general judgement is made about their essay-writing ability. A series of tasks on a range of topics can become a portfolio, which is likely to lead to superior information about student ability compared to a one-off examination.

Indeed, markers too can be influenced by tasks or topics, though this is generally small.[60] Nonetheless, it is useful to consider whether scores are affected by how much the marker loves or hates the topic being scored.

Markers

Brennan[60] has reported that marker effects are small in large-scale, high-stakes marking panels that are tightly trained and monitored: certainly, what was achieved in the New Zealand norming of student writing for Grades 5 to 12.[54] However, in low-stakes, small-scale marking in school classrooms, there is potentially a large disturbance in marking. Markers tend to be highly variable throughout the marking process, partly because judging complex products requires considerable mental effort over a long period of time to ensure marking is finished promptly and to a high standard. Markers get fatigued, and sometimes cynical, and start taking short-cuts in the scoring that result in drift from the standard. The impact of an uncomfortable chair, poor lighting or heating, lack of food, consumption of alcohol, tiredness, or change of mood can all increase variability of scoring. A number of important mitigating practices have been identified:

1. Markers need to attend to all aspects of the task in light of the demands made in the instructions. A generic rubric may need to be modified to ensure the specifics of the task or topic are incorporated into the marking scheme.
2. The use of at least two markers for each essay will reduce error greatly. Although this increases work, double-marking or check-marking of just a sample will raise credibility in the marker's judgements. It is worth remembering that the score assigned to student work ought to be credible to a colleague as well as to the student and their family. If questioned about a grade or score, teachers are in a stronger position to defend their grading if they have already come to a common understanding of quality.
3. Increasing consistency of marking can be done by marking all work on a similar topic before starting on other work. This reduces the possibility of a halo effect (this student did well on Topic 1, so they will do well on Topic 2) and instead allows the marker to compare like with like.
4. If it is possible to mark all work on a topic in one sitting, the marker should do so. Marking is less likely to drift if not interrupted. However, if work can't be marked all in one go (e.g., breaks for meals or sleep), then the marker should

recalibrate their internal standards. This involves recording the scores given to a set of three to five tasks without making any notes, ticks, comments, or ratings on the tasks. Then, as a new marking session is started, those tasks should be remarked. If ratings are very close to original scores (e.g., $+/-1$ score) then it can be argued that internal judgements are on the same wavelength as the previous session. Of course, if the scores are wildly different, then any notes taken in the previous session need to be reviewed to see how or why the marking has deviated. If the marking cannot be brought back in line with previous scoring levels, then a serious problem exists that will probably require further training and support before making any educational use of these scores. This may be embarrassing, but it is better to face this inconsistency in judgements than conduct invalid assessments and disseminate unreliable grades or data to students.

5. The identity of the student doing the essay usually has only a very small impact on a marker's scoring.[60] Knowing that the essay was written by one's star pupil may tempt the marker to inflate the grade, but this tends not to be the case. Most markers would not consciously introduce such blatant error into their scoring. Removing identifying information about the student before marking is possible in formal examinations, but nearly impossible in classroom marking. Hence, in classroom settings the marker needs to avoid the appearance of favouritism while appropriately awarding high marks or grades to high-quality work. At the same time, the marker should avoid adjusting the score for the work by what the student can do in another context or at other times. Only the work at hand should be marked. However, teachers still have the possibility of commenting on the work as to how it compares to previous or other work.

THE ESSAY

Having introduced and explained rubrics, let us look now at essay question assessment. Essays have been used prolifically for a long time—the earliest examinations of some 3,000 years ago in Imperial China were written essays.[63] In most content areas that use essays, students will be expected to engage in a certain cognitive task (e.g., discuss, compare, contrast, or analyse) in relation to a certain set of content (e.g., the causes of World War I, the impact of the setting on a character's development, or the role of mutation in disease). Such prompts can usually be crafted quite quickly and focus student attention on important cognitive and curriculum objectives. The real work in an essay is in the scoring.

Most essay examinations require students to write a cogent response to a task or prompt that they have not previously seen, and they must produce this response on demand at a certain time and place (there is no going away to look things up and finish tomorrow). Furthermore, contrary to good writing practice, the essay written in an examination is a first draft—it has not been read by a peer, no feedback has been given, and no external tools for editing or proofing were allowed. This means that the essay writer has to have internalised all the writing processes and be their own critical colleague, editor, and proofreader. With the time pressure and the high-stakes nature of essay examinations, students generally do not produce their best work. Thus, the essay examination will probably not represent fairly or accurately the full range of a student's writing ability or thinking. Nevertheless, many people consider essay examinations to be powerful evidence of higher-order thinking processes and profound understanding of valuable content.

Unfortunately, evidence exists to suggest that essays are not actually measures of higher-order thinking and deep knowledge. In a now famous study of more than 1,000 essays, Ellis Page[64] compared the scoring of six humans and that of a computer program. To score the essay, the computer program used variables intrinsic to the language of the written essay, such as grammatical accuracy and vocabulary size and rarity, and various approximations of quality, such as the length of the essay and the ratio of active to passive voice verbs. The average correlation of agreement between the computer and the six humans was higher than the correlations obtained between the six human judges. In other words, regardless of what the humans thought they were doing when they scored each essay, there was a huge language component in the way they assigned their scores—otherwise their scores would not have resembled those of the computer program. Since then, advances have been made in automatic essay scoring and all such advances make use of the same language components of essay scoring.[65] Thus, because scoring an essay may be a response to language skills rather than substance, there is a confounding interpretation of essay scores.

To reduce the impact of language and surface features on interpretations of written essays, it may be useful to redesign the essay task so those features are reduced in their influence.[58] For example, providing all students with a common framework of starter sentences or organisational headings would ensure that markers are less influenced by stylistic features rather than content or logic. Alternatively, Shavelson, Ruiz-Primo, and Wiley[66] have shown that instead of writing an essay, the completion of a concept map in a topic area can both be scored reliably and also validly demonstrate that students have a deep understanding of a topic area. These approaches create a much fairer basis for determining what students really know and can do by cancelling out the impact of language skills and features. Certainly, under examination conditions, these techniques would probably generate better quality writing.

PORTFOLIO ASSESSMENT

Portfolios and e-portfolios are becoming increasingly commonplace in classroom assessment, especially in higher education. A portfolio of artefacts creates the potential for a systematic, purposeful collection of student work documenting achievement and progress across time.[67–69] Despite great advocacy for portfolio use, there is little evaluative research that identifies success and failure factors in their usage.[70] Nonetheless, a portfolio, digital or otherwise, gains learning power when students are required to make made purposeful selection from a body of work and provide a rationale or justification for why each piece has been selected. This is akin to the work curators of art galleries or editors of volumes carry out when they select pieces for a collection and when they produce an introductory piece in which they draw attention to the organising themes and messages being highlighted through their deliberate selection.

The successful portfolio depends on an effective collaboration between the learner and the teacher. Although the goal is that students take ownership and responsibility for the contents of their own portfolio, they are dependent to a great extent on the greater understanding the teacher has as to the future requirements and uses of the portfolio. Thus, students need motivation and a sense of efficacy, alongside scaffolded support by the teacher, to fulfil the purpose of a portfolio.

Clearly, the metacognitive processes involved in selecting and justifying selections for a portfolio require critical thinking and self-reflection, skills that develop with input from the teacher. Since this is a valued educational outcome, portfolios may be implemented just for their pedagogical impact with scant regard for how they should be assessed or evaluated.

With increasing access to multi-modal computer-based e-portfolio technologies (e.g., Google Sites, MyPortfolio by Mahara), and increasing instruction in the use of them, e-portfolios can incorporate sound, moving images, hyperlinks, networked documentation, and cyber-objects. Initial research with university students has suggested that attitudes towards the technology components of an electronic portfolio system do impact on how students perceive and, potentially, perform on courses that are evaluated in part with a portfolio,[71] though alternative e-portfolio systems may not differ much in terms of capability or student attitude.[72] Portfolio use for assessment is viewed positively by students.[73] Nonetheless, there is workload which may be more easily handled in an e-portfolio (provided teachers have the technical know-how to operate e-portfolio systems) that needs to be taken into account.

However, portfolio use does not automatically create deeper academic abilities.[74,75] Furthermore, because portfolios require considerable work both for students to create them and teachers to provide meaningful formative feedback, their use does not guarantee efficient delivery of useful formative feedback and can interfere with completing other courses.[75] Nonetheless, some positive outcomes have been found with portfolio use, including better academic writing, deeper reflection, and greater creativity.[76]

Four main types of portfolio have been noted:[67] (a) the working portfolio, which provides a comprehensive record of all work being done as it is done, (b) the showcase portfolio, which exhibits the culminating achievements of a learner, (c) the evaluation portfolio, which provides evidence related to qualifications requirements, and (d) the class portfolio, which reports student classroom activity to administrators, parents, and other interested parties. The power of an e-portfolio, over the traditional physical artefact collection, is that curation of contents for new purposes should be much easier. Nonetheless, there are challenges when working with portfolios of any kind.

A working portfolio contains all the work a student does, whether it is finished or not, without any attempt to select or censor its contents. For students it is useful to have a place where they can deposit partial work that keeps a record of ideas or roads not taken because these can inspire future directions or potential. Fundamentally, students need something to draw on for future uses. However, in this condition the contents are uncurated and unlikely to provide useful information about student thinking and learning. Assessing a working collection simply gives an indication of how diligent students had been in populating the portfolio. A challenge for many students early in a course is seeing the importance of putting things in the portfolio; lack of motivation and attention early on may generate regret when formal evaluation processes expect a curated, well-thought-out collection.

The point of the display is to demonstrate the highest level of achievement or effort or ability for use by an external, usually prestigious, audience. Ideally, the student selects the work from the various pieces in a working portfolio that shows off the student's skills, knowledge, or ability in the best light. For example, the music student may have a large repertoire of practice pieces (including scales), but only a few pieces that really show their expertise. Most importantly, a display portfolio needs a written or video-recorded statement that gives the rationale for the selection. This metacognitive reflection forces the student to engage in the deepest and most complex aspects of learning.

The purpose of an evaluation portfolio is to document that a student's work meets the expected or specific outcomes of a course of instruction or a qualification (e.g., AP Studio Art). The portfolio shows that the student meets the expected objectives of the evaluation. The audience is normally an external agency (e.g., Board of Graduating Teacher Standards) which awards qualifications according to set criteria and processes. Again, the student has to select, from a working portfolio, those works which most clearly exhibit the required characteristics set out by the qualifications agency. Some evaluation portfolio systems require the student to include some work that shows progress from initial draft efforts through to completed, and to provide reflective commentaries on the items selected and how they meet the required criteria.[77] Again, a reflective essay integrating the various components may also be required.

A class portfolio is a summary collection of work done in a class and is used by the teacher to demonstrate to parents and administrators what the students have done in class. Again, the student, possibly with the teacher's instruction, will select those pieces from a working portfolio that most clearly exhibit what the student has been doing. The portfolio may contain a summary sheet outlining its contents and relating them to the important targets or learning intentions set for the class. The teacher may contribute to the class portfolio by providing a set of notes that draw the reader's attention to the salient features of the portfolio as they relate to the classroom instruction for that child. Clearly, a great deal of time and effort is required to compile the information, especially if students and teachers have not been diligent in capturing it during the course of the year.

Assessment Challenges With Portfolios

Assessing a complex product as a portfolio requires considerable thought as to what the educational goals are for the collection. Specifying those goals (e.g., meet qualification authority requirements, demonstrate growth and development, etc.) needs to be done early in the piece so that students can come to grips with what it is they have to achieve with the portfolio. One model for achieving this can be seen in the teacher education PROVEE.IT model.[78] This model puts students in instructional teams (IT) to plan (P) the purpose of the portfolio (i.e., product or process focus) and reflect (R) on the types of evidence needed to fulfil the purposes. Students then express their opinions (O) as to appropriate criteria, set values (V) for the scoring rubrics, and decide how they would evaluate (E) the portfolio and evaluate (E) the process used. Such an approach depends strongly on mature, motivated students who can insightfully specify how the portfolio should be judged. More commonly, students express frustration at not knowing exactly what is required of them.[76]

Nonetheless, portfolios are especially dependent on the amount of time taken to create them, which can lead students to a loss of motivation to persist and complete them. Designing and implementing a portfolio-based teaching and learning environment requires considerable work by the teacher compared to the simplicity of administering tests. Further, American research in the 1990s, during the height of enthusiasm for using portfolios to assemble evidence of student learning, demonstrated that the reliability of scoring was much poorer than objective testing. Thus, rubrics that align to the appropriate curriculum expectations, standards, and functions of a portfolio are highly recommended as a beginning point to evaluating portfolios. It is worth noting that this alignment is necessary, since students and markers ought not to substitute a large, voluminous portfolio with one that is slim but contains high-quality reflective statements and rationales. The guidance given earlier in this chapter about moderation and standards of agreement need to be applied here also.

An example of high-stakes, high-quality portfolio assessment is the American AP Studio Art evaluation.[77] The AP Studio Art course is examined with a portfolio in which students demonstrate in one of three domains (drawing, 2-D design, or 3-D design), three major facets of art (i.e., quality, concentration, and breadth) regardless of the medium. To make management of objects feasible and to enhance comparability, all portfolios consist of a set of photographic slides that are rated by examiners to determine the degree to which the student has shown the three facets. All portfolios—between 7,000 and 10,000 per year—are brought to one site for rating. An elite team of 25 readers or markers, all experienced in studio art and trained to score according to the AP rubrics, rate each portfolio for one of the three facets and each facet is marked by two or three judges. The portfolios are laid out on large tables and each reader walks down the line, inspecting the slides for a facet, and gives each portfolio a score, ranging from 1 to 4 for just that facet. At the end of each table, the scores awarded by the reader for that set of portfolios are entered into a statistical software package for monitoring consistency between readers and also to determine the reader's tendency to be lenient or harsh. Anomalous readings are drawn to the attention of the chief reader, who can investigate and adjudicate a final mark for the portfolio. In the event a reader is consistently at odds with the other readers, retraining can take place, and in extreme circumstances, readers who do not improve their accuracy can be let go. The identification of consistently harsh or lenient readers is conducted so that their marks can be statistically adjusted. This ensures students are not unfairly disadvantaged by harsh markers or unfairly advantaged by lenient markers.

Similar procedures are carried out in other jurisdictions, especially in the studio arts and design technology disciplines. Rigorous portfolio scoring processes are expensive and time-consuming, but essential to establish and maintain credibility in the judgments. Unless quality processes like the ones described here are followed, it is difficult to believe that portfolio assessments are credible. In conclusion, portfolio assessment is a great idea, but is really hard to do properly.

AUTHENTIC ASSESSMENTS

Schooling itself is an artificial environment; it is not the adult world in which the knowledge and skills being taught will be used. School assessments, thus, are inherently artificial—but paper-based tests (especially multiple choice) seem even more removed from the reality in which students will need to function. Hence, efforts in the last few decades have been made to increase the realism and authenticity of school assessments. The goal in this approach is to make the student think, learn, and perform in a manner that is similar to the real world. Some subjects are more obviously authentic (e.g., courses in cooking, driving, and workshop come quickly to mind), but creative minds have tried to make assessments in all subjects more realistic. Needless to say, the success of such activities depends on the methods by which the quality of student responses are judged.

Authentic problems are relatively ill-structured and poorly defined, in contrast to well-structured tasks that predominate in formal testing.[23] Such tasks force the learner to figure out what is going on before attempting a response. Information literacy requirements[79] and technologies allow the generation of authentic tasks based on complex real-world problems. For example, McKenzie[80] suggests the following authentic task that requires students to make use of official weather data for a number of cities resulting in a recommendation based on various climatic factors and personal preferences:

> A science teacher who has been leading his middle school classes through a study of climate wants his students to appreciate the difference in weather patterns between various cities and towns in [←*insert country name*→]. He might ask them to select a city in which to live . . .

The proposed benefits of authentic assessment are manifold. In the authentic activity, the learner has to construct meaning in a relevant and relevant environment. This is considered to be highly motivating because it connects students to what they already know and wants to learn. Solving such realistic problems is also how skills within a discipline develop: we learn by doing, as well as by reading or watching. Performance on realistic activities also provides rich, powerful feedback to teachers about who needs to be taught what by allowing the instructor to see not only what a student does but also how the student does it. This clearly makes a lot of sense in vocational and professional preparation, and these are areas in which the secondary school assessment systems excel—if an assessment of motor mechanics does not require fixing a car for real-life clients whose day will be ruined if the car breaks down again as soon as it is driven from the garage, then the assessment is not authentic. Clearly, the pedagogical implications of authenticity are immense and speak to the need to collect information about learning in the most direct way possible.[31] However, issues to do with the validity of assessment of authentic practices are not easily addressed.

There is no suggestion that only authentic assessments can and should be used. Indeed, insisting on only authentic assessments in such high-risk occupations as dentistry, surgery, or flying could have hugely negative consequences for students and their willing authentic clients, who could be harmed should the student make a mistake. Nevertheless, the surgeon wanting to master heart bypass surgery will need to be assessed, not just with computer simulations and quizzes on proper procedure, but also with the real McCoy. Trainee surgeons may work their way up to the procedure—first watching, then helping the master, then doing it under close supervision, and then finally, being assessed solo. If the patient does not die, the patient's quality of life is improved, and the heart remains bypassed—and if the surgery was done in an efficient, competent manner—then the surgeon has passed the evaluation. Distance from the real world is what authentic assessment is trying to reduce.

Fortunately, we have authentic pedagogy in schools around technologies, performing and visual arts, and practical skills. The way we teach writing—with brainstorming, drafts, readings, rewrites, and publication—mimics the authentic world of how a writer's work is created and published. Furthermore, how we assess the stages of the writing process can mimic the real world if we make use of the portfolio system and rubrics. Consider how we score art by having students do art; how we evaluate dance by having students dance; how we assess foreign languages by getting students to have a conversation in that language rather than to translate lengthy written passages; or how we assess oral rhetoric by having students give speeches. Authentic assessments for school students need teachers to creatively imagine scenarios in which the students can interact as real-world experts and professionals might. Further, in authentic tasks, attention can be paid to not only what is produced (the performance or the product) but also to how the learner goes about doing the authentic task. Close inspection of the process might generate powerful task-oriented feedback for the instructor and the learner.

Contrast these authentic assessment activities to the kinds of seat-work assessments we conduct in the more traditional academic subjects. In mathematics, we may assess student performance on measurement by their ability to make appropriate calculations based on a given scenario, but that is some distance from going outside and measuring the length of a shadow and angle to the flagpole before conducting calculations to determine the height of the pole. But authentic assessment is about more than doing assessments in the real world; it is also about giving students assessment activities that matter in the real world. This has brought much emphasis to embedding subroutines into the realities of practical life. For example, instead of simply asking children to solve $75 - (75 \times .125) = x$, we embed the problem in a scenario that involves extracting from a situation the critical information and determining the appropriate procedure: Johnny wants to buy a pair of shoes that cost $75 (tax included) before the shop offered to pay the sales tax of 12.5% for him. How much does he need to pay? This is considered closer to authentic because it is the type of real-world situation that the student may actually encounter. Of course, it is unreal in so many other ways: Where's my calculator? Where's the shop assistant who explains the deal? Where's the shop till that automatically calculates the correct price? Nonetheless, getting students to do activities that involve realistic behaviours and which can be part of our assessment arsenal is a good thing. The Authentic Assessment Toolbox (http://jonathan.mueller.faculty.noctrl.edu/toolbox/index.htm) is a tutorial for learning about authentic assessment. It is presented with hypertext and features for creating authentic tasks, rubrics, and standards for measuring and improving student learning.

However, let us not get carried away by the allure of authenticity. Our problem as instructors and teachers is a simple one: if a student can't do our authentic task, does that mean they can't do the skill or they don't have enough knowledge of the authentic context to be able to respond appropriately? There are clearly alternative explanations that may threaten our desired interpretations. In the sales tax example, it is clear that the ability to read matters and the prior knowledge of what sales tax is and how much it might be may also interfere with a student's ability to conduct an assessment. The instructor may get a false reading of what non-English-speaking-background students know mathematically because of the authenticity factors of the task. Hence, when the curriculum calls for embedding mathematic or scientific knowledge in realistic, authentic scenarios and tasks, teachers must temper their assumptions about student knowledge by the role that literacy or cultural knowledge plays. Thus, our pursuit of authenticity may jeopardise our ability to interpret and respond to student learning needs appropriately.

Clearly, in any given time period, it is not possible to collect as much information about a student's learning through authentic tasks than is possible by administering paper-and-pencil questions. Authentic tasks take time to do, let alone time to create. Students cannot do many activities in a time period, so our sample of their domain knowledge or ability is restricted and the consistency of scoring between raters is complicated by having both the product and the process to consider. Thus, getting reliable scoring on authentic activities is highly problematic.[81] Additionally, because authentic activities require interacting with real-world objects and processes, they can be expensive to create and run, which creates challenges within a school.

So the solution to the promise and the weaknesses of authentic assessment is not to throw it away or ignore it. Rather, by combining multiple assessment methods, it is possible to guide instruction based on a rich understanding of students' strengths and weaknesses. Remember our description of the multiphase driver's licence examination system that involves initial paper-and-pencil testing followed by multiple authentic on-the-road assessments. The authentic judgments are strongly guided by a specified set of tasks and standards of performance administered by a trained professional judge. In school settings, the goal is to replicate the authenticity of the experience, including the authenticity of the evaluative processes, with the added agenda of using those authentic assessments to provide details to the learner and the teacher as to what skills need to be developed and which have been mastered. It is highly admirable to include real-world activities, contexts, and purposes in the assessment of school learning.

In looking back across this chapter, there have been many references to using technology-enhanced assessment practices (e.g., e-portfolios, digital exemplars, computer simulations). It is worth noting that computer and Internet technologies are becoming increasingly part of educational assessment, especially in the design of new methods of test delivery and scoring, and especially in high-stakes qualifications or certification assessment.[58] As these penetrate into classroom practice, as suggested in this chapter, new issues will arise in ensuring students are adequately prepared to cope with these novel assessment methods[76] and that teachers themselves are competent technologically to handle the requirements of assessing with technology. Thus, the deployment of technology enabled assessments needs to occur hand-in-hand with good teacher preparation.

Four

Involving Students in Assessment

The logic of involving students in assessment practices is remarkably simple: if students understand the criteria and standards by which their own work products, portfolios, or performances will be evaluated, they will be better able to regulate their own learning processes.[23] When students understand the learning intentions or goals and the progress indicators used by school and society, they ought to be able to critically reflect on their own work and that of their colleagues. Hence, student involvement in assessment is intended to lead to improved learning. This is one of the defining characteristics of the strongly pedagogical understanding of assessment for learning,[48,82] though the assessment qualities of such practices may not meet conventional standards.[46] In a strongly pedagogical view of assessment for learning, students obtain motivating feedback from themselves, their peers, or their teacher. This feedback informs and enables their learning, otherwise the assessment has not been formative. Beyond the development of self-regulation and deeper understanding of quality, involving students in assessment raises the potential for more feedback, which is a potentially powerful contributor to achievement.[33] Teachers by themselves are unlikely to provide enough feedback to each student and so making use of peers to provide useful insights to students is very attractive. More feedback can arise by having the individual student reflect on their own work (i.e., self-assessment) and by having the student's colleagues or peers provide critical evaluations of each other's work (i.e., peer assessment).

Student involvement in assessment is not new. In the area of English language arts, students are frequently asked to grade—perhaps informally by clapping—the quality of their peers' performances in oral language performances (e.g., debates, dramas, or speeches). Additionally, students have been asked to write reflective journals in language classes in which they were expected to evaluate the qualities of their own work products and processes. Involving students in rubric creation and usage in language arts has also shown that students have a grasp of what is required that aligns well with external standards.[83] Furthermore, in many student-centred primary school systems, students are actively encouraged to set their own goals and review their progress towards those goals in teacher—student conferences. Project learning activities in schools make frequent use of group work and peer assessment as part of the learning process. Indeed, portfolio assessment, especially, requires students to purposively select from their own work for inclusion. These authentic and curriculum-appropriate activities certainly require students to have a deep understanding of what is required and how to judge their own work and that of their peers.

However, research has made it clear that students do not automatically share our enthusiasm for student involvement in assessment, nor do they automatically trust their peers.[37,38,84] Students have concerns about the lack of content expertise that they themselves and their fellow-students have, the emotional and psychological consequences of publicly disclosing one's weaknesses, and the inability of student assessment to assuredly identify how deficiencies can be improved. Thus, while it is important that learners engage in thinking about quality relative to their own learning, there are psychological and social challenges when students become involved in assessment processes. The goal of this chapter is to examine more critically what is involved in self- and peer assessment, and involving students in assessment.

SELF-ASSESSMENT

Self-assessment is the process by which students describe their own learning products or learning processes in light of agreed characteristics and standards.[85–89] Sometimes, self-assessment involves assigning a merit attribution (i.e., is my work good, so-so, or poor?) in addition to the descriptive analysis of the features of work. Self-assessment involves monitoring one's own work and providing feedback to oneself as to strengths, weaknesses, and next steps. Self-assessment is a complex, metacognitive process, which, despite the label, is an evaluation of one's own work, not oneself. While self-assessment is embedded in self-regulation of learning, it is not automatic that participation in self-assessment leads to greater motivation or self-regulation,[23] though some studies do show that such benefits occur.[85]

Empirical work has shown that most novices and younger children make overly optimistic and unrealistic self-evaluations of their own work, while more expert and older learners tend to make value judgements about the qualities of their work that correspond with those of their test scores and teacher evaluations.[85,87,89] While optimism about our capabilities might help us overcome various setbacks in learning and daily life,[90] being overly optimistic or pessimistic might lead to invalid decisions about one's future. For example, youngsters who are influenced by achievement stereotypes (e.g., ethnic minority students are not good at mathematics[91]) might choose not to pursue further opportunities in mathematics despite good performance on tests. In contrast, consider the many young people who believe they are talented singers and end up making fools of themselves at talent shows or karaoke events. Unfortunately, humans are inclined to use inappropriate standards by which to evaluate their work. It is well-established that we tend to overestimate how quickly we can do things, we overlook crucial information, we may protect our standing in society by dissembling about our abilities, we tend to value effort we have made over the quality of our work, and we tend to compare ourselves favourably against others.[92] It has also been established that students use heuristics that can lead to a false sense that they have learned something, including reliance on inaccurate prior knowledge, or dependence on memory of items studied previously.[93,94] Developing a realistic self-assessment may mean becoming less optimistic about one's abilities, which should not be considered failure.

Unsurprisingly, then, students have to be taught what to focus on when evaluating their own work. Coming to a realistic appraisal of the quality of one's own work requires clarity in knowing what the standards are for evaluating work. We generally evaluate the realism of student self-assessments against their performance on tests or the judgment of teachers. Correlations between the self-evaluations of school-age students and teacher ratings or test scores generally range between .20 and .40, with few exceeding .60.[85] These are not strong associations, meaning that the different sources of information generate divergence.[32] Indeed, the insights available from self-assessment, even if discrepant to the teacher's perspective, offer interesting opportunities for teacher-student discussion and—especially if a weakness has been identified by the student—an opportunity to provide customised teaching.

The teacher must make sure that students understand which aspects of performance are important and how to recognise quality or progress within those aspects.[85] To do this, the teacher must have sufficient content knowledge to be able to teach realistic self-evaluation processes. Just as important, the teacher needs to have a curriculum and teaching resources for introducing students to the importance of being realistic and to develop the skill of realism with increasingly more complex learning outcomes.[93] Students seem to develop realism in self-assessment when they have opportunities to practice in formative contexts that provide feedback as to the believability of their self-assessment, and possibly when they are rewarded for honest self-appraisals that do not paint their work in a glowing light that it does not deserve.[87,93] The good news is that, with training in self-assessment, there are increases in learning and academic performance.[85]

An interesting challenge exists for teachers who ask students to self-assess. While the teacher has the responsibility to improve student outcomes, the student may feel uncomfortable in divulging a self-assessment that is either negative or highly personal.[37,84] If pressured to reveal an unflattering result, the student may understandably give a dishonest report. For example, students will indicate greater understanding than they have if they fear the teacher will be angry at them or if they fear disapprobation from a classmate.[37] Since one of the goals of self-assessment is to build self-regulation, allowing students the right to privacy in their self-assessments seems necessary, at least some of the time.[84,87,88] Another challenge for self-assessment revolves around student autonomy. While teachers and courses may require students to self-assess their work relative to stated and explicit course goals, there is a case to be made that students may evaluate their work relative to their own personal, but legitimate goals.[89] The criteria students use to evaluate their learning may be relatively incidental to stated goals, but deeply important to themselves. Since self-assessment is done by and for the self, it may be inappropriate to question such evaluation.

Nonetheless, there is strong similarity in the tertiary sector[95] and the school sector[85] as to factors that increase the realism of student self-assessments. The more concrete a learning objective is and the more objective scoring tends to be (e.g., spelling, science, or engineering), the more student self-assessments are similar to the assessments of teachers. Greater consistency between students and teachers is found when students self-rated their knowledge of traditional academic outcomes (e.g., knowledge of facts or details in a subject, ability to do specific skills), rather than when they were asked to evaluate their own professional practice (e.g., teaching practicum). The level of internalisation of assessment standards used by clinical or professional experts to judge the quality of practice is not evident within students' judgements. Student self-assessments are more like those of teachers or tutors when students use an absolute assessment against fixed criteria/standards rather than comparisons made on a relative basis to the performance of other people. It seems easier to say 'my work is X' than to say 'my work is better than that of Y people.'

Thus, self-assessment is a complex process requiring a delicate hand so as to maximise realism. It is all too easy for students, for many reasons, to avoid realism, and it is up to teachers to provide training and infrastructure that permits useful self-assessment.

Examples of Classroom Self-Assessment

Tools for self-assessment can help turn this advice into something practical. Following is a sample of general approaches that may be useful beginning points. It is worth remembering that interpersonal and psychological trust are necessary, otherwise pressure to be unrealistic increases.

Self-Marking

Teachers have long had students mark their own or their peers' homework or test answers by calling out or showing the correct answer and having students mark whether the answer was right or wrong. This, at least, teaches students to be realistic or accurate in their marking. However, to go beyond objectively scored items is a major objective in conducting self-assessment. In this case, students would be given model answers, ideally annotated with commentaries, and a rubric against which they evaluate their own work. The evaluation could be a judgment as simple as worse, about the same, or better than the model, taking advantage of skills humans have in making comparative judgements.[63] Students would then be asked to give reasons or justification based on similarities or differences to the model answer for why they marked their own work as they did.

Clearly, some preparation is needed to ensure relevant annotated exemplars and rubrics are available. It also means that the annotations and rubric need to be available to the student in language that the student can appreciate and use. Something written for a teacher may be of little use to a primary school student. Regardless of whether the plan is to use the student mark for reporting or recording purposes, or to generate feedback to the student as to the realism of their marking, the teacher has to review the student work and the self-marking, then generate an adjusted mark or feedback. This is an opportunity to help the student further understand what the criteria in the rubric and exemplar really mean in contrast to their own work.

Self-Rating Inventory

Another option is to give students a series of questions or prompts against which they rate themselves. Many student self-rating forms and schedules have been developed and all follow a somewhat similar format. The student is presented with a task, statement, or question and asked to rate themselves using some sort of scale. The scale could be dichotomous (like me—unlike me) or it could offer a multi-step scale of responses (e.g., a balanced Likert scale or an unbalanced, positively packed scale). The students may be asked to rate themselves against a variety of criteria (e.g., frequency, importance, or level of agreement). The developers of such self-rating inventories may provide norms against which student performance can be evaluated or may even provide critical scores which alert the teacher to an important learning need or strength. Care needs to be exercised to encourage students to rate themselves as honestly as possible. Exposure of such self-ratings to parents, the teacher, or other students may discourage honesty.

Class-Generated Criteria

Instead of just giving students a rubric as a *fait accompli*, it may be possible to generate appropriate assessment criteria for an assessment activity with the students themselves. Students are often extremely aware of what quality looks like in any important learning domain. With judicious prompting by the teacher, a class-made scoring rubric can be developed.[83] The students then use the rubric to develop a critique of their own response to an assessment activity. Several studies have reported that involving students in the development of criteria led to more accurate self-assessments and learning gains.[85] To ensure the development of realistic self-assessments, the students have to use the criteria to evaluate their own work and have that check-marked by the teacher, who can use discrepancy to stimulate a potentially rewarding discussion with the student. The focus initially could be on whether the student has used the criteria realistically rather than how good the piece of work is.[93] In higher education, it is reasonably well-attested that more experienced and senior markers are more lenient than tutors or new academics,[54] so it should not be a surprise that students may be harsher on themselves than the teacher would be. After establishing that students use the criteria realistically, grades or marks for the assignment could be awarded for doing the activity itself.

Traffic Lights

This is a simple self-assessment where students show the degree of their own understanding by displaying a coloured traffic light.[96] Green indicates full comprehension, yellow suggests partial or incomplete understanding, and red indicates a serious deficiency or weakness in understanding. Because this is a public process, teachers should remember that some students may be reluctant to display their own lack of understanding in such circumstances.[37,84] Public usage requires the development of classroom environments that encourage and reward honesty. The responsibility for this falls on the teacher, who must exhibit appropriate responses when students fail to comprehend.

Whatever light is displayed, students should be asked to provide evidence or reasons for their light selection. If done privately, this information could be cross-marked by the teacher. Perhaps the learner needs to be told '*yes, you really do understand this*' or '*unfortunately, you still misunderstand this part.*' Some students, due to personality characteristics, will tend to overestimate their abilities, while others will tend to underestimate theirs; this is when the teacher's personalised response can help the student see their own work in a more objective light. Whatever the individual feedback, the teacher can use the self-reporting information to identify which students need to be taught what content. Nonetheless, without appropriate levels of trust, students have been found to lie on their traffic light self-evaluations for fear of making the teacher angry or being shamed by a classmate.[37] Great care is needed when self-assessments are disclosed publicly.

Judgment of Learning

Judgment of Learning involves students in predicting how well they will do on a forthcoming test of the material being studied.[97] Subsequently, students' actual performance is compared to their predicted self-assessment of how many questions they would get right. This is a prospective monitoring of future performance in contrast to retrospective monitoring of previous performance, which is more commonly how self-assessment is conducted in schooling.[98] A clear advantage of this technique is that it provides an objective measure as to whether the student's prediction was accurate and realistic. However, it depends on having the type of learning material easily suited to objective testing. Hence, this technique may be useful early in the process of teaching students how to be realistic in their self-assessments.

PEER ASSESSMENT

Peer assessment is the appraisal of student work by fellow learners.[99,100] This requires each student to produce a critical analysis of someone else's work and to receive critical appraisals of their own work. This interpersonal process involves exchanging a performance evaluation so as to give and receive feedback from others aimed at enhancing the performance of an individual and/or a team or group as a whole.[101] Peer assessment requires students to be explicitly interdependent in that they agree their peers are competent to judge, and they are willing to receive feedback, while they themselves pledge to do their best in giving and receiving feedback.[102] Avoiding the many problems of group work is essential[102] (e.g., all the work done by one person, credit is given to undeserving group members) to ensure quality peer assessment. This matter dominates much of the concerns adolescents and young adults have around peer assessment.[37,38,84,101]

Marking a classmate's test score or homework sheet is a long-standing peer assessment process. However, to get at deeper learning outcomes, peer assessment requires guided judgements about the qualities of a peer's work, in the same manner as teacher judgement of student work and student self-assessment. Clear, agreed-upon scoring criteria or rubrics, supplemented by annotated exemplars, are essential tools. The goal of peer assessment is rich feedback to a peer about the strengths and weaknesses of the work, using a guided marking sheet or rubric. The awarding of merit grades should be treated cautiously, as there is conflicting evidence about the effect of this. Generally, if teacher grades have a negative impact on learner performance,[103] then grades from a peer are unlikely to be useful.

The assignment of work to peers has to be considered to avoid overly friendly partners or enemies whose marking may be distorted by the social relationship; there is evidence that peers do tend to overrate their friends' work.[104,105] Nonetheless, a group of Hong Kong tertiary students indicated they would give their friends helpful comments in response to poor-quality work, while lying about the grade they would award,[106] suggesting that friendship groups might be useful if formative commentaries as feedback, rather than evaluative grading, are sought.

Again, there is an important role for the teacher to moderate peer judgements. Students accept that their classmates may not be as insightful as a teacher,[37,38] and they accept that teacher moderation can be a way for the peer evaluator to get constructive feedback about their own assessment or evaluative abilities—sometimes the peer assessor needs to learn in what way their assessment was endorsed or rejected.[38] Certainly, because there is the possibility of friendship or enmity contamination in any grade or score assignment by students, use of such grades or marks has to be tempered by the teacher's greater expertise in the field being assessed. Once the teacher has reviewed the peer assessment, the power of peer assessment is fulfilled when the teacher and peer feedback are returned with the assessment activity to the author of the work.

One variation of this—perhaps most useful for in-class presentations or performances—is to have students use a holistic rating scale to score the quality of a performance as an adjunct to the teacher's evaluation. A holistic scale is preferred since there is usually not much time between presentations and so an overall impression is appropriate. A possible scale might use quite colloquial but vivid language, such as for lowest (*I was confused or bored*) and highest (*I enjoyed and learned so much*). Again, moderation by the teacher will reduce the possibility of friendship or enmity marking. Nonetheless, without justification of the ratings, such assessments are unlikely to help students develop a deeper understanding of quality characteristics. A somewhat more advanced peer assessment mechanism is PeerWise (https://peerwise.cs.auckland.ac.nz/). In PeerWise, students deposit multiple choice questions on a topic being studied by a class. Classmates enter the shared space, attempt the questions, and give feedback to the question authors as to the qualities of the item, including debating the correct answer.

Like peer tutoring and peer group work,[102] peer assessment can develop a range of abilities. In order to be effective within a classroom environment, peers have to develop the ability to work cooperatively and to not make personal attacks.[101] Seeking constructive, critical feedback from one's friends and peers seems to be a good way to develop the quality of a learning environment; students may be more honest and informative than teachers simply because they are more accessible.[38] Peer assessment develops self-regulation in that emotional discomfort, fear of possible ethical violation, and interpersonal relationship challenges all have to be controlled in order to give and receive feedback comments.[101] It appears that students who handle these challenges best will gain the most from the peer assessment process,[101] thus, teachers need to create environments in which psychological safety and trust are maximised. This means that the environment has to prioritise a common commitment to giving and receiving honest commentaries without attacking or feeling attacked.[101] A shared set of values and reasons for peer assessment has to be established. This can be seen as similar to the reasons for having an honour code about not cheating.[24] Initially, anonymity in the peer assessment process may allow students to develop confidence in giving honest feedback without fear of recrimination.[101] Teacher moderation in early stages would help eliminate egregious and unnecessary ad hominem comments and ensure a supportive environment is created. Nonetheless, feedback from a peer encourages the development of a formative mentality around assessment; an assessed activity is seen as an opportunity to expose one's own mistakes for improvement, rather than as an opportunity to be punished for failure.

Furthermore, peer assessment helps students develop metacognitive insight into the characteristics of quality work by requiring them to conduct an examination of the strengths and weaknesses of a peer's performance. To do that, the cognitive skills of evaluating, justifying, and using discipline knowledge are needed. Of course, in its simplest forms (e.g., using a holistic rating scale), few of these skills could be developed. Instead real benefits occur when students have to identify and justify their assessment of peer work.[101] It is generally accepted that engagement in this kind of peer assessment produces better learning for the student who conducts peer assessment.[101]

Implementing peer assessment requires significant upfront preparation on the part of the teacher. The teacher must be able to convey clear instructions to students as to how the assessed work is to be delivered to peers, how to evaluate the peer work, and how to return the peer work with the appropriate feedback.[105] Then, there must be an actual mechanism for physically moving the assessments between and among students. Dissemination and handling of peer assessments can be assisted with through electronic tools such as shared work spaces (e.g., e-portfolio systems) or by email. The teacher requires a recording system to know who has which work to evaluate. This is necessary to ensure that everyone gets the same number of pieces to assess and to ensure that there are no habitual assessor–assessee pairs which might lead to invalid processes. Also a mechanism is required for archiving assessed work and peer evaluations for possible auditing, especially if the peer assessment is going to count towards a summative grade. Archiving may seem unnecessary to teachers who wish to prioritise the formative feedback function of peer assessment, where the benefit is seen in the interaction between assessor and assessee.[101] Perhaps, instead students could self-archive their own work in a portfolio system, along with the various peer assessments associated with the work. Such a process would help students to reflect on evidence of progress, improvement, or even persistent challenges in their learning.

Falchikov and Goldfinch[105] provide pertinent recommendations for use of peer assessment in school contexts.

1. Keep the size of the peer groups doing assessment of peer work small (maximum of seven). Besides requiring considerable time taken from other activities, having to do a lot of assessments tends to make peers less reliable and consistent with how teachers or tutors would assess. Such reduction would discredit the validity of peer assessment to all stakeholders.
2. Like self-assessment, keep the focus on traditional academic school content, rather than on complex practices (e.g., practice teaching).
3. It has been found that when the peer rating is restricted to an overall holistic mark rather than multiple dimensions, peer assessments reflect more closely those of instructors. Nonetheless, such an approach reduces engagement with complex criteria.
4. Well-understood rubrics and/or criteria are essential.

5. Involvement of students in the design of, or discussions about, rubrics or criteria leads to greater similarity in judgements between peers and teachers.

An embedded theme through all this discussion is the importance of rubrics. Without a shared understanding of what the curriculum or teacher expects and what progress looks like, students cannot be taught to, nor can they actually practise, self- or peer assessment. Additionally, students need training in how to be realistic in their analysis of work so that their judgments become more like those of the avowed experts: the teachers. The psychological safety of the interpersonal environment is paramount. No matter how promising it is to involve students in making judgments about their own or peers' work, it will all be for naught if they do not trust themselves or each other. Further, student involvement in assessment requires the teacher to be an active participant in the whole process: designing tools, environments, processes, and checking and moderating. The teacher must teach students how to evaluate work against criteria and act as the quality assurance mechanism. Assessment for learning involves students, but does not exclude the teacher.

Five
Feedback, Grading, and Reporting

The goal of teachers and students making all these judgments is to generate insights for teachers and students as to the successful attributes of work, any deficiencies, and possible actions that could be taken to further improve the work. Simply, this is feedback. However, this is not the noise heard when the output sound of a loud speaker is channelled back into the input microphone (a circular causality loop). Rather, this is a combination of corrective and evaluative information about aspects of one's performance or understanding.[107] Jargon terms such as 'feed up' and 'feed forward' have been introduced to indicate different roles that feedback can take. However, the key common questions in all feedback models are: (a) What are the goals the work is trying to fulfil? (b) What are the current characteristics of the work? and (c) What needs to be done next by the teacher and/or the learner?[107] While some might suggest that without a formative response that leads to improvements by the learner feedback is just information,[108] it is certainly clear that without the descriptive information there can be no potential for using the feedback.

The responses that teachers make to learners verbally in-the-moment and, more formally, in writing about strengths, weaknesses, qualities, standards, expectations, goals, and so on comprise feedback. Feedback is generally a powerful key to learning gains,[33,107] but not all feedback is equally effective for all students in all situations.[103,108] It is also worth noting that feedback is actually automatic since students receive feedback from their own internal judgments, emotions, and physical responses to assessment events.[109] This type of internal feedback is outside the direct control of teachers but will certainly have an impact on student reaction to external feedback such as test scores, grades, or comments. Students who endorse the value of feedback are likely to achieve more because they see feedback as an aspect of their self-regulation.[110] Hence, the power of feedback is determined, in part, by whether students believe in using feedback of any type as a useful instrument in the self-regulation of learning. Getting students to believe this is, naturally, an important role for the teacher.

It matters that students engage with feedback and that teachers give high-quality feedback because the overall impact of feedback on learning outcomes is positive and among the largest influences on achievement.[33] Hence, in terms of teacher responsibilities, effective feedback is one of the most powerful interventions a teacher can implement.

PRINCIPLES OF FEEDBACK

In keeping with notions of validity, feedback has to provide a defensible interpretation of performance on a task that leads to appropriate decisions about what is next. We also need to remember that much feedback is given in class on-the-fly, which means there is a strong possibility of it being off-the-mark or inappropriate—but it will be timely. More considered feedback can be seen in written comments on course or homework, written reports sent home, or in parent-teacher conferences. These may provide a more coherent evaluation, but will be somewhat delayed. Like assessment, there is no perfect feedback.

Current thinking about feedback depends heavily on the Feedback Intervention model[110] which focuses on first identifying a discrepancy between desired and current performance with the intention that the individual work effectively to close the gap, rather than abandon the goal or reject the feedback. Classification of the focus of the feedback identified that there were four possible options (i.e., the task, the processes needed to do the task, self-regulation mechanisms, and the self).[108] Based on this classification, it has been established that all but self-focused feedback leads to increased learning outcomes. Self-oriented feedback (e.g., praise and personal evaluations—*Good boy!*) tends to distract the learner from the requirements of learning growth and instead focuses attention on the ego. Efforts to protect or maximise the ego can prevent learning growth.[111] Just as self-assessment must focus on the work, not the person, so must feedback focus on what is needed to do the task, not the person doing the task.

A New Zealand study of how students experienced feedback suggested that teacher-dominated practices (i.e., comments for improvement, teachers helping, and teachers evaluating) were endorsed more than student-student feedback, and that high school students focused more on teacher evaluation feedback than primary students, who emphasised teacher improvement comments.[112] An examination of the written feedback comments New Zealand students gave to each other and themselves showed that task-oriented feedback dominated.[113] Interestingly, self-oriented feedback decreased in self-assessment with increasing grade level, while it increased in peer assessment, suggesting that older students were less concerned with protecting their own egos but more concerned to maintain positive relationships with their peers. A Singaporean study effectively taught chemistry students to generate peer feedback that moved away from dichotomous (accurate vs. inaccurate) to more comments focused on task, process, and self-regulation.[114] Additionally, a national survey of New Zealand teachers showed that teachers strongly believed feedback was given to improve student outcomes, though primary teachers endorsed the use of peer and self-feedback much more than secondary teachers, who indicated they used more protective evaluation techniques (i.e., couching poor results in self-oriented affirmations).[115] Students have expressed frustration with feedback that does not specify how to improve, even if the feedback is laudatory.[38] The knowledge of how to improve and what to improve has to come from the teacher, who clearly knows more about the task and the process than the learner. Hence, in the school systems examined here, student experience of feedback depends—perhaps rightly because teachers are more expert than students—on teachers giving constructive comments and students giving themselves or peers task-oriented feedback advice.

Given these types of beliefs about feedback, it is expected that good-quality feedback should be relatively widespread. However, teachers must have a clear understanding of what they really want learners to be able to do, know, and understand (i.e., curriculum). The clearer those learning intentions or targets are to the teacher and the student, the more feasible powerful feedback will be. It also means that teachers and students need a reasonably accurate depiction of where student performance in terms of the desired skills, knowledge, and understandings actually rests. Since all assessments are to some degree error prone, that means the knowledge teachers have is imperfect, though it improves by addressing the challenges described in this book. Finally, for feedback to be effective teachers need to have clear understanding of what

Feedback, Grading, and Reporting 77

needs to be done to close the gap or discrepancy between the current location and desired destination. Teachers thus have to have extensive pedagogical content knowledge[116] of how to support, coach, or direct a student to move on from wherever they happen to be to the next stage of progression. This is clearly a difficult challenge, and it is understandable that many students lack the ability to give such advice.

This type of feedback is actually harder than it sounds. For example, consider the learning intentions of a teacher of early literacy who seeks to ensure children master the conventional narrative story schema by reading stories to them. The teacher will draw to the students' attention the order of events and the kind of things that need to be presented at the beginning, the middle, and the end of a story. In other words, without burdening children with the metalanguage, teachers want children to know, recognise, and produce appropriate story grammar. In order to determine whether children have met that learning intention, the teacher creates an assessment task that states: *Write a story that makes sense all the way through.* In response, imagine a child writes the following story.

> Thre pigges builded howses frist one wuz strw, scond wuz wud and thrid wuz brik The bad wufl blue down the strw and wud howses the pigges randed to the brik hows the wufl kudnt blo down the hows he climed down the chimne and diedied in the fire the pigges wuz happi

What feedback should the teacher provide? Many may react negatively to the poorly constructed surface issues of grammar and spelling and this would lead to feedback that focuses on those features. But such a response misses the fundamental insight that the writer has met the learning intention. The story makes sense all the way through if you read past the surface errors. Thus, the teacher can report to the child and the parent that the student has met the learning intention. Additionally, the teacher has identified a new objective that will require some instructional input—spelling! But that new learning target should not take away from the fact that the student has met the stated learning intention.

It is vital that teachers make and keep public the real learning intention *and* stick to it when devising feedback for each student's performance. Otherwise, children will learn very quickly that teachers do not mean what they say and will focus on meeting the hidden curriculum—*all the teacher wants is neatness and accuracy*. When confronted with performances like this Three Little Pigs story, the best response seems to be to make public that the story meets the intention, and to privately engage with the student to focus on the extra learning intention.[117] Thus, good feedback is precise, descriptive information on current status relative to learning intentions followed by advice as to progress.

Note that this is not the same as praise or blame. Effective feedback is not a person-oriented evaluation. Rather it is a description of the task or process relative to clear criteria and prescriptive as to appropriate next actions. Praising a 5 year old for writing the Three Little Pigs story highlighted earlier or shaming an 11 year old for the same story will not inform either child as to what they need to do next to improve. 'Well done' and 'could do better' do not belong in the lexicon of teachers when they give feedback to students or to parents. Feedback must identify what could be improved and offer directions as to how to improve.

The text box provides excellent advice addressing things to do, things to avoid, and contingencies to consider in giving feedback.[102,107,118]

Feedback should	Feedback should not
• focus on the task, • be presented in chunks the student can handle, • be clear and straightforward, • be honest and objective, • focus on learning goals, • maximise dialogue between feedback giver and recipient, • focus on positive aspects of performance, • be conducted in a warm and supportive manner, • be congruent with what students have been told to expect, or • specify specific action(s) that would lead to improvement.	• compare students to others, • give grades in most instances, • use praise in most situations, • rely on oral feedback, • focus excessively on analysing errors, • overwhelm student with errors, or • mix evaluation of performance with criticism or praise of attitude or behaviour.

In terms of tailoring feedback, it seems best to:

- adjust timing to the difficulty of task—sooner for hard tasks, later for easy;
- use immediate feedback for procedural or motor skills;
- delay feedback to promote transfer;
- delay feedback for stronger students, but give it sooner for weaker students; and
- give more indirect feedback to stronger students, but more specific feedback to weaker students.

Thus far, I have focused on how to give feedback based on a judgment of the qualities of student learning. There are more formal processes of feedback that need to be addressed; that is, giving grades or scores and reporting to families or administrators. These two administrative functions introduce additional challenges for feedback.

Grading

As mentioned in Chapter 3, evaluating student performance on a quality scale is almost a universal practice. While some jurisdictions outside the United States do not use letter grades (e.g., New Zealand's 'Not Achieved' to 'Excellence'), the alternative systems have many of the same functions and challenges as grading has. Students, and many parents, have a legitimate expectation that the teacher will report using a grade or mark system to evaluate the quality of student work. Parents also expect feedback as to their child's attitudes, behaviour, or participation in school activities to have a rounded sense of the child's schooling experience. Hence, teachers have to generate meaningful summaries of the complex experiences students have in any period of time. This is made more difficult by the reality that childhood and adolescence are periods of rapid growth and development, and sometimes of great *Sturm und Drang*.

Grading of student learning and communication of those grades are difficult, especially when they attempt to summarise multiple sources and kinds of information into a single indicator.[119] Research on letter grading has clearly shown that a major problem is the inability of teachers (as report-writers) and parents (as report-readers) to give the same interpretation to a grade. For example, a US study[120] found that parents thought a C was acceptable, representing an average amount of achievement, while teachers used that grade to indicate a poor or unacceptable level of achievement. Further, it is common in the United States[121] for teachers to adjust grades student-by-student so that a letter grade does not mean the same thing for all children. For example, a capable student who has been misbehaving in class may be given a C as a warning, while a very weak student who has tried very hard but failed to produce what was expected may be given a C to motivate continued effort. Is it any wonder then that some parents may be inordinately proud of a C in the latter case, and others shame-faced and furious about the C given to their otherwise stellar student?

In addition to the communication problem in reporting achievement, there is the problem that teachers often do not agree with each other as to what level of performance constitutes a certain type of grade. Part of the disagreement is inherent to human judgements—we have different abilities to recognise important features of work, we have differing expectations, we have differing experiences. Part of the disagreement can come about because of practices such as averaging across quite different content or subject matter (e.g., your final grade is based on your performance on a one-hour test of mathematics, a five-minute speech in English, how well polished your woodwork project is, and everything else you did).[121,122] Clearly, averaging of data across such diverse sources is a problem, especially when there is no agreement as to the relative weights of the component assessments. In other words, should the mathematics test carry more weight in the final overall score than performance in woodwork?

Related to this is the problem of how to properly account for work that should have been done but wasn't or work that was completed late. Teachers and schools need consistent policies and clarity in communication to students and families as to how late or incomplete work will be handled. Nonetheless, the policy has to resolve how late or absent material relates to the quality of the work that was actually done. What kind of grade describes brilliant work done on time, three pieces missing, and another late, but well done? What implications are there if an A grade is given because of the quality of the work, despite missing pieces, when other diligent students have done competent, but not brilliant, work on all five pieces which were submitted on time? Is it honest and fair to say that one is an A and the other a B? Is it better to penalise the first student for incomplete with a D? Or should the first student be given more opportunities to complete the missing work? And if we take that option, what consequences are there for teacher workload and student equity? Clearly, averaging and aggregating across different kinds of work and different statuses of work is problematic; hence, the recommendation to state the rules in advance and keep the reporting of what is done separate from what is not done.

Another major source of inconsistency between teachers is something that has already been alluded to: the blending of academic performance with attitude or effort.[121–123] This means that actual achievement scores are moderated by the teachers' perception of how hard the student tried and/or how much the student has shown positive regard for the teacher or subject. This response is not restricted to teachers: parents sometimes want the reported achievement to be adjusted for non-academic aspects. There are parents who might suggest lazy, but very able, students should not get an A, but there are probably more parents who believe their hard-working, less able student merits an A. This problem is not restricted to compulsory schooling: even higher education students have pressured for better grades based on effort rather than quality of work,[124] even when formal grading criteria focus on the product and not the student's effort. Much as students, teachers, or parents may want to exercise therapy in the construction of achievement grades, the meaning and power of reporting is clearly diluted when achievement is mixed with attitude or effort or any other aspect of schooling. Separation of academic performance from effort and attitude in creation of grades appears to be relatively commonplace practice outside the United States, and may change within that country with the introduction of standards-based curricula.[125]

One option in response to these difficulties with grading is to avoid achievement grades altogether (no percentile, no percentage, no stanine, no grades, no scale scores, no curriculum levels, no age-equivalents, etc.). Instead, teachers could replace them with longer narrative reports that describe the various achievements and performances of the student. As might be expected, a large number of people might not like this—employers want something easy to grasp, parents just want to know if their student is doing well or not, and teachers might not want to have to write long reports. Manageability and desirability are both problematic if we choose to abandon grades, but communicability and accuracy in reporting may also be jeopardised if we insist on using grades. Research in the United States has shown that parents and administrators preferred long reports with many tables and graphs but that they actually more correctly interpreted long two- to four-page narrative-style reports.[126] Frankly, graphical reports without supporting text are too prone to misinterpretation. Not providing grades has been shown to lead to deeper engagement of students with substantive feedback, so there is a case to be made for this practice.[102]

Thus, grading, to be meaningful, has to make clear what it contains and how it is derived. A system that all stakeholders understand and agree upon is essential if grading is to contribute to improvement.

Reporting

Grades by themselves are not the end. School systems globally require teachers to report formally about students and their learning. Quite frequently reports go beyond academic achievement, including such things as behaviour in class and on the playground, attendance and tardiness, aptitudes and interests, attitudes, effort, extra-curricular activities, and so on. Principles of good feedback discussed earlier apply here.

New Zealand research into teacher reports for parents has identified that there is a tendency to focus on surface features (e.g., presentation, neatness, quantity, and effort) and a tendency to praise the learner with positive comments such as 'Doing well for his age' or 'A pleasure to teach'.[127] A problem with this type of report, despite its optimism, is that it denies information to parents if there is a problem that needs to be addressed—which is something parents desire and are entitled to know.[128] One supposes that this optimistic report may be received more favourably than one that blames the learner for not studying or working hard. However, the purpose of reporting, like feedback, is to cause a change in home-based practices that would lead to better performance, and so honesty, clarity, and supportiveness are necessary.

A reason for glossing over problems and being positive in reporting to families is a fear of blaming or labelling the child or inadvertently threatening the well-being and self-esteem of the child. This child-centred concern may be more evident in Western nations. Indeed, American students were aware of when teachers had 'pulled their punches' in giving feedback, grades, or reports and were dismissive of the impression management teachers were exercising.[129] Teachers may have inadvertently subscribed to an ego-protective approach to assessment and feedback rather than a growth-oriented pathway.[111] Keeping reporting focused on the principles of feedback will help keep reporting focused on growth.

In accordance with principles outlined already, a key way to interpret and report performance is to compare it with appropriate curriculum standards and criteria being used to guide teaching (*criterion referenced interpretation*). A second approach (*norm-referenced interpretation*) is to compare student performance to how well others similar to the student are doing (e.g., rank-order position in class, grade, or normal distribution). A third comparison is to contrast current performance with one's own previous performance (*ipsative-referenced interpretation*).

Norm-referenced interpretations involve comparison with other people on the assumption that knowing where a person stands relative to others could be useful. Knowing a child is in the top three or 10 of a class, not only indicates the student is doing well, but also brings honour and prestige to the child and family. Unfortunately, in every ranking someone has to be last, and half are below average. This understandably elicits quite different emotional reactions. A problem with rank-order scores is that small differences in actual ability can reflect large differences in rank, with invidious results. Remember the difference between first and last in an Olympic race is often a small difference in time, while the difference in rank suggests a large difference in performance. This means that relative to criteria, all finalists in the 100 metres have performed very well and all have compared to the average person, but according to rank-order scores, there are only three winners (Gold, Silver, and Bronze) and many losers. This same problem applies to rank-order scores like those seen in international comparative test systems.

Ipsative-referenced scores are commonplace in tracking and monitoring activities like sports or weight loss. Seeing change in the desired direction can be motivating. However, small changes might not represent differences beyond chance. *Value-added measures* have to do with how much increase in achievement data can be attributed to the efforts of a school and are a kind of ipsative comparison. However, it is difficult to infer causation when there are many chance factors (e.g., unreliability of measurements or ratings, maturation differences, teacher or school changes, etc.) impacting on achievement.[130] Another complication arises when trying to determine if students near the top of a scale have improved when there is little room to improve.[131] For example, going from 90% to 95% is a small gain compared to a student who goes from 50% to 60%. However, if the ratio of gain to maximum possible gain[132] is examined, the first student has gone up 50% of the maximum 10 marks possible while the second has gone up only 20% of the possible, indicating that perhaps the first student has added more value than the second, despite the difference in raw score gains. It should also be evident that gains are not linear; learning of complex skills takes considerable time and pathways to improvement often contain plateaus, rapid gains, unfortunate regressions, and random deviations.

Given these problems with norm-referencing and ipsative-referencing, there is general consensus that a report should describe current status. A good report describes—like good feedback—where the student currently lies on the progression with a description of strengths and needs. As in grading, a good report separates important characteristics (e.g., attendance, achievement, attitude, effort, etc.) and ensures that end-users understand them appropriately.[133]

Six

Objectively Scored Assessments

Assessment, most commonly, invokes the idea of written questions or items that can be scored objectively; that is, there is only one right answer and the identification that the test-taker has supplied that answer is certain. The most famous of these is the multiple-choice question, which can be scored by a machine, giving extremely high reliability in awarding marks to students who have chosen the correct option. There are two major classes of objectively scored assessments (i.e., selected response and brief supply). Before discussing these it is important to overview why teachers and assessors use this type of task.

Objectively scored tasks are used because their marking is extremely efficient and accurate. Further, students can answer many questions quite quickly (usually one multiple-choice question per minute) and responding is so simple that test-takers do not need to write. This quickly generates a large sample of ability within a learning domain, leading to a strong ability to accurately discriminate among students as to who has more or less knowledge, ability, or proficiency. Additionally, when students see the correct answer as a choice, it actually raises their overall achievement; it is easier to recognise the right answer than generate it. A further strength to objective scoring is that it engenders a sense that the testing is fair since the opinion of the individual marker is not used to evaluate the response.

Needless to say, there are disputes as to the virtue of objectively scored tasks. Although there is an objectively correct answer, the selection of the content to be tested and the phrasing and framing of the question is not objective.[134] This means that sometimes such tasks prioritise material that is easy to test this way, instead of valuing important material in the curriculum. It also means that the way the task is written may cause confusion or ambiguity. Thus, devising such questions is difficult, and there are a number of common errors made when writing such tasks that allow the test-wise student to get items right even with relatively little knowledge. Whenever a student has to choose the right answer from among a set of possible answers, it is possible to get the item right by chance, even if the task is well written. This means that the score can be inflated by chance, which is much less likely when the student has to create or supply an answer.

Objectively scored tests require careful attention to the writing of instructions and options. In addition, tests must be carefully designed to ensure the items provide appropriate coverage of the desired content or curriculum domain. This chapter will briefly outline conventions and rules-of-thumb for creating or evaluating a variety of objectively scored item types. These rules and procedures have been developed to ensure that, when a student gets an item right or wrong, interpretations are legitimate (i.e., getting an item right means the student actually knows or can do whatever the question assesses). If there are other explanations for a wrong answer (e.g., the item is poorly written), then any interpretation or decision is likely to be invalid.

TEST DESIGN

A well-designed test ensures that items cannot be answered correctly based on errors made in item writing or test construction that reveal what the right answer is or allow elimination of wrong options. Too many students are capable of doing well because they are aware of the kinds of error made in the design of objectively scored tests. For example, a common test-wise piece of advice is 'when in doubt, guess Option C.' This advice is effective because too many test developers put the correct answer in Option C, rather than ensuring that correct answers are systematically and relatively equally distributed across all positions. There are many other pieces of test-wise advice that this chapter has taken into account.

A standard solution in devising an objectively scored test is to plan the number of questions and their type for each content area or cognitive skill that needs to be covered in order to achieve confidence that students know or can do what is being taught or what is required. A plan is essential to ensure that all the tasks and items are appropriate to the content area (i.e., no items outside of the intended teaching sneak into the test) and of an appropriate style for the content being assessed. This plan is sometimes known as a 'template' or 'blueprint' and guides item writers as to how many items of which type are needed for each content depending on the purpose of the test. A second advantage of the test template is that it allows the organization of items into meaningful groups so that feedback and reporting focuses on the construct being sampled, rather than on performance on each item. It is much more useful to discuss student performance per important teaching or curriculum objective than to talk about how each student did on Question 13.

For example, in a classroom test of 45 minutes that covers mathematics material taught in the previous four weeks, it might be useful to limit the test to somewhere between 30 and 40 items, so that speed of answering is not being tested. Given that number of items, and the need to probe a skill or knowledge area with enough items to come to a reliable summary of performance, it seems likely that at most four topic areas could be covered ($30/4 = 7.5$ to $40/4 = 10$ questions

Objectively Scored Assessments

Table 6.1 Possible Objectively Scored Test Template for a Classroom Test

Content area	Item Formats			Cognitive Demand		
	MCQ	Complete Equation	Short Answer	Recall	Transform	Total
1. Multiply whole numbers	4	2	4	6	4	10
2. Multiply decimal numbers		5	3	4	4	8
3. Multiply fractional numbers	4		3	3	4	7
4. Multiply percentages		5	5	5	5	10
Total	8	12	15	18	17	35

per topic). Hence, a template would specify what topics will be included in the test, how many items will be on each topic, and what types of question formats would be used, and it would guide how feedback and reporting is done. Table 6.1 is a possible test template for a 45-minute test in multiplication.

Other aspects that need to be considered in planning an objectively scored test include:

- The difficulty of the items is appropriate to the curriculum expectations and the teaching that the students have received.
- The items cover a range of desired cognitive skills.
- All items are expressed in language suitable to the abilities of the students being tested.
- The answer for any item is not inadvertently revealed in another item.

- The correct answers are known and unequivocally correct.
- There are clear rules for scoring any short-answer questions.
- There are clear rules for allowing students to be legitimately exempted from the test.
- There are clear rules as to what equipment or aids students are allowed to use.
- It is clear that students have experienced the item formats previously.

These issues matter since weakness in any of these areas reduces the validity of any interpretations and actions,[40] even if the test can be scored reliably and quickly. It is also the ethical and professional obligation of classroom teachers to check that any objectively scored tests they are asked to administer meet these expectations.[135] Otherwise, the time given over to use of the test is actually time wasted from working on intended outcomes.

SELECTED RESPONSE ITEM FORMATS

A number of item formats require the test-taker to select from a list of options providing the correct answer. This section illustrates key features of these item formats.

The Multiple-Choice Question

Multiple-choice questions (MCQs) were developed to overcome the unreliability inherent in judging the quality students' written answers. MCQs are frequently used for factual recall or simple understanding, although they can be used to test deep cognitive processes as well as creativity. MCQs can be used:

- wherever a single, clear answer is called for;
- when the range of possible correct answers is very large; or
- when coverage of a wide range of material is required.

A good MCQ has a question or set of instructions (the stem), the correct answer (the key), and plausible wrong answers (distractors). The stem should present a clear and concise statement of what the student is being asked to do or think about. The stem should not be too long to read or understand. The best stems are those that are phrased as questions (What is the name of this tool?) or as instructions (State the name of this tool.) rather than as run-on sentences that need to be completed (The name of this tool is _____.). There are many correct ways of completing a sentence which are not what was expected or intended (e.g., The name of this tool is hard to remember.) and do not demonstrate the expected knowledge.

Good stems keep the focus on the desired learning, rather than draw attention to material that students are not expected to know or use. Hence, phrasing the stem negatively (e.g., Which of the following was **NOT** committed in New York City?) is highly problematic educationally, let alone linguistically or psychologically. Answering negatively worded questions invokes different skills than responding to positively framed tasks, commands, or queries.[136] However, if it is absolutely necessary to have a negative element in the stem, it is imperative that the negative element is emphasised, perhaps with different font formatting (Which is **NOT** the name of the capital city?). This technique gives test-takers a better chance of noticing what they are being asked; hence, interpretations are more likely to be valid.

The key is the one clearly identifiable correct option. If plausible arguments can be made for more than one option, then MCQ is an inappropriate format. There can only be one answer for which credit is given. The item writer ought to submit the draft item to others to check that the key is the key! There is no substitute for multiple-checking by other people who also know the content. The key must be a concise answer that will satisfy a qualified judge as being a correct and adequate answer to the question. The response should not answer more than what the question asks.

Distractors are the wrong answers which should appeal only to the student who knows little, has a significant misunderstanding, tends to guess, or tends to not try. Each distractor must (a) appeal to some sort of misinterpretation of the material that students commonly exhibit, (b) call on an overgeneralisation of the content, or (c) be caused by unsound reasoning. Good distractors may repeat some partially true part from the stem or associated stimulus material, but such repetition should be only partially related to the correct answer. Distractors may be statements that are too broad or too narrow to be fully correct, or they may sound plausible to an uncritical or inattentive student. Based on classroom experience of mistakes that students make, the teacher can predict a series of errors and the kind of wrong answer that might result. The number of options required in an MCQ is conventionally between three and five. More options tend to reduce the power of guessing, but adequate discrimination has been found using as few as three options.[137]

For example, Figure 6.1, using social studies as the context, shows the kind of thinking needed to develop distractors that might legitimately attract a student with less than full knowledge or understanding.

Each distractor is a highly memorable date related to British, European, or New Zealand history and each date has the key numeral 2 in it, so partial memory of that number is not helpful. Note also that the options have been arranged in a chronological order to reflect the time series. This simplifies thinking about the task by removing the demand of a jumbled

> **Which year is most associated with the early European exploration of New Zealand?**
> **a)** 1215
> (This year is the signing of the Magna Carta; a significant date in Western history but not directly New Zealand history)
> **b)** 1492
> (This year is associated with Spaniard Christopher Columbus' arrival in North America)
> **c)** 1642
> (correct – This year is when Dutchman Abel Tasman is first recorded sighting what he called New Zealand)
> **d)** 1852
> (This is the year the New Zealand Parliament was constituted, but is not related to its exploration)

Figure 6.1 Sample Social Studies Multiple-Choice Question

order, meaning that error was not caused by an extra skill not being tested. Note also that 'all of the above' or 'none of the above' were not used. These are generally not very discriminating options, since the test-taker needs to find only one exception in order to eliminate this option.

Getting an MCQ item wrong should alert teachers to an interesting result: the student does not know something that has been taught or is being planned to be taught. This error should validly inform teaching practice and should not be caused by poor item writing. It is clearly the item writer's responsibility to ensure that all the obvious causes for incorrectly answering the item are removed, and teachers should check this before administering the test. Since educational assessments ought to align with curricular goals, not intelligence per se, anything that distracts from that curriculum objective is not appropriate.

Objectively Scored Assessments 95

To appreciate the power of being test-wise and the consequences of poor item writing, answer the MCQ test in Figure 6.2. Each of the questions has a logical or 'best' answer from its corresponding multiple-choice answer set. 'Best answer' means the answer has the highest probability of being the correct one in accordance with the information at your disposal. There is no particular clue in the spelling of the words and there are no hidden meanings. The answers are at the end of the chapter, but please complete this test before looking at them.

This exercise shows how poor item writing can invalidate the information that MCQs provide. High scores on this test do not mean test-takers understand 'fradric'; instead they mean test-takers are test-wise. Thus, test users and test creators need to review all items before using them to make any educational decisions. If the test can be answered correctly without knowledge of the taught material, then the teaching was not necessary and the test does not measure the effect of teaching.

A criticism of MCQs is that they assess surface thinking only. This is really a function of item writing quality and test design more than anything. If stems and options are crafted to demonstrate analysis, critical thinking, or even creativity, then MCQs can elicit evidence of higher-order thinking. Inferential reasoning can be evaluated with MCQs, provided items are well written. Excellent examples and advice on writing MCQs exists in many standard texts that are continually updated.[138–141]

Mix-and-Match or Unequal Lists

A useful variation on the MCQ is the mix-and-match or unequal lists format, which requires connecting material from two lists (Figure 6.3). This technique is ideal when

1. The nonoxyonized fradriç will klavužů best with an
   a. gloin
   b. haradrů
   c. lembed
   d. oxstypnæ ( )

2. The lembed frequently overglozus the haradrů because
   a. all lembed are beyonzé
   b. all lembed are always onderzu
   c. the haradrů is usually snickered
   d. no haradrů is gložable ( )

3. Palantír is present when
   a. harad snickers the gloin
   b. the schnazz-gul overglu, if the gloin is onderzu or beyonzé
   c. the gloin overglus
   d. etherlrids gložu easily ( )

4. The purpose of the schnazz-gul is to generate
   a. schnazz-gloins
   b. etherlrids
   c. haradrim
   d. schelob-gloins ( )

5. The reasons for nonoxyonized fradriç are
   a. the oxstypnæ overglu with the lembed
   b. few haradrů were accepted in schelob-gloins
   c. most of the gloins were onderzu
   d. the lembed beyonzé and the haradrů snickered ( )

6. Which of the following is/are always present when schnazz-gul are being snickered?
   a. grozu and gloin
   b. fradriç and gloin
   c. gloin
   d. gloin and oxstypnæ ( )

7. The klavužů function of the oxstypnæ is most effectively carried out in connection with
   a. haradrů
   b. the nonoxyonized fradriç
   c. the beyonzé schelob-gloins
   d. a onderzu lembed ( )

8. _____
   a.
   b.
   c.
   d. ( )

Figure 6.2 A Test of Best Practice in Writing Multiple-Choice Questions

> **Match the French word with its English equivalent.**
> Write the letter of your answer in the space to the right of the numbered word.
> Each word may be used once or not at all. Each item is worth 1 point.
>
> **French**
> 1. bras _____
> 2. tête _____
> 3. dos _____
> 4. jambe _____
> 5. nez _____
>
> **English**
> a. mouth
> b. head
> c. back
> d. front
> e. arm
> f. leg
> g. hand
> h. nose

Figure 6.3 Sample Mix-and-Match Item

objects (e.g., authors, theorists, places, vocabulary) have to be matched to appropriate definitions or examples. By making the answer list longer than the question list, the probability of getting each item correct by chance is lower, including the last item left in the set. This would not be the case if the lists were of equal length. The answer list probably should have two items more than the question list. The challenge can be increased by requiring double matching; for example, match the theorist and the concept to a series of definitions or statements.[142]

Sequencing

Sequencing is a selected response item in which material has to be put in logical process order or sequence (Figure 6.4). The skills of being able to put things in order is important in many

98 Objectively Scored Assessments

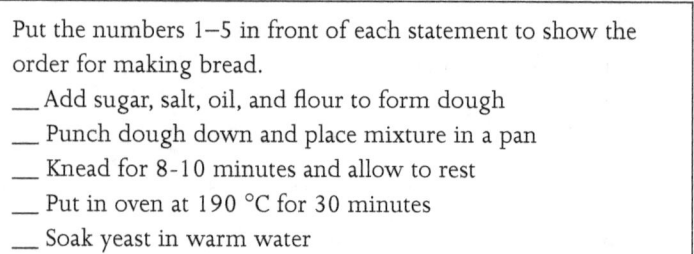

Put the numbers 1–5 in front of each statement to show the order for making bread.
___ Add sugar, salt, oil, and flour to form dough
___ Punch dough down and place mixture in a pan
___ Knead for 8-10 minutes and allow to rest
___ Put in oven at 190 °C for 30 minutes
___ Soak yeast in warm water

Figure 6.4 Sample Sequencing Format

curriculum statements. The design of such tasks is straightforward, but the conventional scoring of 1 point for each item in the correct position is problematic for students who misplace items. If the relative order is preserved despite the error, the conventional approach will give a low score suggesting the student knows little, when this is probably not the case.

A more sensible scoring procedure is to work out the discrepancy between the student answer and the correct answer.[142] This involves determining what the maximum wrong discrepancy value could be if each answer were in the most wrong position it could be (e.g., last and first swapped). Using this as the divisor, the student's discrepancy from the correct can be determined and used to calculate a proportion of the score awarded for the sequencing task. For example, in a 5-point sequence like Figure 6.4, the most discrepant score possible (i.e., getting every item wrong by the step furthest from it) would be:

1st step is put in 5th position = 4;
2nd step is put in the 4th position = 2;
3rd step is put in the 1st position (position 5 is already taken) = 2;

4th step is put in 2nd position = 2;
5th step is put in 3rd position = 2.

This gives a total of 12 as the divisor. If the student swapped only the first two steps (i.e., 2–1 instead of 1–2) and got the remaining three in the right order, the discrepancy would be 2 because each of the two wrong answers was wrong by only one position. Thus, the score would be (12 − 2) / 12 = 10 / 12 = 83%. With this type of scoring it is possible to award part marks in accordance with the relative competence of each respondent.

However, it is unlikely that a simple sequencing task of five items could be worth 12 marks. A common solution is to weight the question so that it is worth fewer marks (e.g., 2 or 3) depending on the importance of the sequencing task relative to all other items. So if the weighted value of Figure 6.4 were maximum 3 marks, 10/12 would be worth 2.5/3.

Binary-Choice Questions

Even simpler than these three-item selection formats is the binary choice task (Figure 6.5). Binary choice simply means the options are dichotomous choices (e.g., true vs. false, right vs. wrong, or correct vs. incorrect).

A clear weakness in these items is that there is a 50% chance of being right, which contaminates any interpretations about

1. If you mix red and blue paint you get green	**True**	**False**
2. Hainan is part of China	**Right**	**Wrong**
3. The femur is in the back	**Correct**	**Incorrect**

Figure 6.5 Sample Binary-Choice Items With Alternative Answer Options

student proficiency or competence. There are two approaches to making these items less prone to guesswork. The first is to require the student to provide a correction if the statement is wrong (Figure 6.6), which reduces guessing for false statements because a correct answer must be supplied in order to get the item right.

The second alternative is to group items around common content and ask students to answer the whole set correctly for the mark (Figure 6.7). Note that this is an efficient method of covering knowledge and understanding around a common topic. At the same time, this format reduces guesswork to at least the same level as a traditional MCQ with four options when only two statements are required to be both correct (½ × ½ = ¼). Figure 6.7 has three statements, so the chance

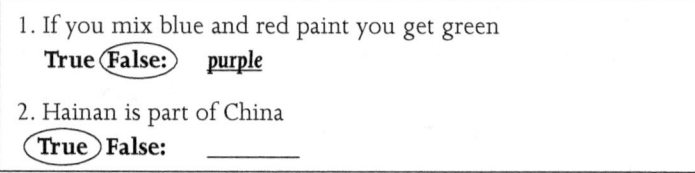

1. If you mix blue and red paint you get green
   True (False:)   <u>*purple*</u>

2. Hainan is part of China
   (True) False: _____

Figure 6.6 Sample Binary-Choice Items With Correction

Answer these three statements about mammals for one mark.		
1a) Mammals lay eggs.	**True**	**False**
1b) All mammals live on land	**True**	**False**
1c) Mammals have hair and produce milk to feed their young	**True**	**False**

Figure 6.7 Sample Multiple Binary-Choice Item

of obtaining a mark by guessing is one in eight, a more demanding standard than an MCQ.

The multiple binary-choice item in Figure 6.7 is cognitively simpler relative to another commonly seen MCQ format, in which the test-taker must choose the option combination that applies to the item (Figure 6.8). The correct answer for the question in Figure 6.8 is (C), but the process of selecting the correct answer involves inspecting and evaluating the combination of options in each answer, instead of simply declaring whether each statement in itself is true or false. This involves an extra step that is not inherent to the construct being tested. Hence, if the item had been structured as a multiple binary-choice, the teacher could be certain that the students knew the material much more directly. A current innovation using this logic, in computer-based testing, is the discrete option multiple choice question, which presents each statement separately and stops the item testing either when the student gets a statement wrong or completes all the items correctly.[143]

A second advantage of multiple binary-choice items is that instead of asking students to identify the one thing that is *not*

Which statements about the Mayan Civilisation are true?
I   Mayan culture is similar to other Mesoamerican cultures
II Mayan religion centered on the linear nature of time
III Mayan writing represented the spoken language
IV Mayans developed an astronomically correct calendar
(A) I and III only
(B) II and IV only
(C) I, III, and IV only
(D) I, II, III, and IV

Figure 6.8 Sample Combination Answer Multiple-Choice Item

true (i.e., Which option is NOT true?), the item can focus more positively on identifying things that are true, rather than false. Since the goals of education include ensuring students learn to distinguish accurate from inaccurate claims or statements and master knowledge about content domains, it seems odd to ask them to identify things that are irrelevant to the domain.[143] It makes much more sense to require students to focus on identifying desired knowledge.

CONSTRUCTED RESPONSE ITEM FORMATS

A number of item formats require the test-taker to construct a response which can be scored easily because the range of possible right answers is extremely constrained. For example, in a simple arithmetic problem (e.g., $7 + 5 = ?$) the correct answer is objective (i.e., there is only one correct answer that all teachers and markers agree on) and, thus, although there is no selection, the item can be scored quickly and accurately. This section illustrates key features of these items.

Insert Missing Material

Being able to insert missing material (e.g., a word, a step in a math problem, a component of a diagram) is an important capability for handling curriculum and life situations. Testing reading ability by asking students to fill in missing word(s) in a text has been shown to be an effective means of evaluating linguistic proficiency.[144] Similarly, items that require the student to complete the missing steps in an incomplete mathematical problem, for example, take advantage of the cognitive benefits of 'worked examples' in which powerful learning takes place as learners borrow from completed examples.[145] Similarly, in more technical fields, asking students to complete a partial diagram exercises analysis, recall, and flexible adaptation to a new context. These tasks require students to pay attention to the immediate local context, as well as global holistic aspects of the gap.

In all three completion tasks, the item must be designed so that only one correct answer is possible, to ensure consistency in scoring between markers and answers. A downside to this approach, of course, is that learners could provide alternatives that are equivalent and correct. Hence, instead of scoring on an 'exact match' basis, an 'approximate' basis could be used—but this would require compiling a list of acceptable answers. An upside to exact match scoring is that, especially, when testing students in reading in a language not known to the tester, a sense of how well the student has done can be obtained.

Highlighting/Underlining

Another objective format, but which involves a constructed response, requires students to circle, highlight, or underline certain parts of a stimulus material or task that contain answers or key points. For example, in teaching punctuation, students could be asked to identify the seven words that need a capital letter in the following: 'tomorrow i will visit the famous golden gate bridge in san francisco.' Identification avoids the necessity of copying out the sentence, which is not the construct of interest. Further, this format seems a more realistic approach to text-editing as a skill than having to choose the correct version of a sentence in a MCQ format.

A challenge for this in paper-based administration, unsurprisingly, is how to score students whose answers are somewhat sloppy and partially identify adjacent, but wrong, words. In computer-based word processing applications, the provision of coloured highlighting should allow this type of item format to be readily implemented, provided students are familiar with the use of such tools. Ensuring accuracy of student selection in these contexts with younger students or those without fine micro-motor skills might require much larger displays or more tolerance in scoring. It is important to keep in mind that by requiring selection or identification of the right answer, the goal is to test curricular knowledge in an efficient manner, while minimising the effect of guessing or test-wiseness.

Short Answers

As I mentioned at the start of this section, it is possible to create questions or tasks that require the production or construction of a brief answer involving a short answer for which there is an agreed correct answer. For example, the name of a famous person, an object, a place, or a numeric value could all be used as a correct response that can be easily scored. However, as in handling completion items, a list of possible right answers may need to be developed because there may be more than one way of representing the correct answer (e.g., $7 + 5 = 12$, or 'twelve' in words, or XII in Roman numerals). Thus, a scoring or marking guide is needed alongside a mechanism for identifying new, but correct answers. The scoring guide also needs to address, especially in the case of written answers, how spelling will be handled: should the correct answer wrongly spelled be marked correct or wrong? Whatever solution to this problem is implemented, it needs to be consistently applied across students and markers, and it needs to be defensibly fair. Marking 'colour' wrong for the word 'color' may be acceptable in the United States, but it is unacceptable anywhere the British spelling is deemed correct.

As in writing MCQs, similar advice on the writing of short answer questions should be followed. Sentence completions

> The president of the United States who solved the GFC crisis of 2008 was _____
>
> *Accept:* Barack Obama; Obama.
> *Exclude:* African-American, angry, frustrated, beleaguered, etc.
> *Rules:* answer must state the surname.

Figure 6.9 Sample Sentence Completion Item

with an open ending might have many perfectly correct solutions which are not in the construct being tested. For example, in Figure 6.9, the intended goal of the question is to elicit the name of the person. However, it is possible to complete the sentence in many novel ways without demonstrating the name of the required person. Hence, writing short answer questions clearly as a direct question would probably be superior (i.e., Which president solved the global financial crisis of 2008?).

If more than one answer is desired (i.e., a list of attributes or characteristics), then the question should clearly state the number of answers expected. This saves the test-taker from having to guess how many answers are required by the test question and helps the student focus on producing the desired knowledge. The importance of a clearly phrased task or question cannot be overemphasised. All questions should be evaluated by a colleague to reduce the chance of ambiguity or lack of clarity. This will improve the quality of the evidence used for making educational interpretations and decisions.

Draw a Shape, Component, or Object

In an extension of the short answer and figure completion tasks, it is possible to ask students to construct a graphical representation of an object. This more likely lends itself to natural and technical sciences where knowledge is often represented graphically and the ability to draw some aspect of that knowledge is necessary: for example, drawing a geometric shape from a set of specifications, a top view of an object from front and side views, an anatomical diagram based on text description, and so on. These type of drawings not only demonstrate curricular competencies but, also, develop cognitive and learning depth because of the requirement to transform an object from one representation to another.[146] Again, the importance of developing scoring rules in advance cannot be emphasised enough. Specifying the correct answer in advance permits development of a valid scoring system.

Measure and Record

Teaching youngsters how to use measurement tools (e.g., rulers, protractors) is an important curricular goal. These skills can be tested, perhaps more readily on paper than on computer screen, by having students use standard tools to measure shapes or diagrams and record their results. Scoring rules are needed to handle exceptions such as answers that are given in centimetres but were asked for in millimetres. Rules will be needed to handle answers that are either insufficiently precise or overly precise (e.g., a kilo is 2.20 pounds at two decimal places, but it is 2.2046 at four decimal places). It is worth noting here that it is important, when items are duplicated for administration, that the intended sizes have been captured on the page. The assessor should check that the diagrams as printed generate the same answers as was intended. This is especially important if the images are reduced so that more questions can fit on a page. Checking the validity of the answer is an important responsibility with this type of assessment task.

CONCLUSION

The examples in this chapter are not exhaustive of all item types, but these are all reasonably straightforward practices that lead to rapid and consistent marking. The items allow coverage of a wide range of useful curricular goals and content. The key is to generate surety that interpretations about performance are not clouded by any inadequacies in the specification of the questions or instructions. Getting the item right or wrong should be a function of the expected knowledge, skill, ability, or understanding—not the result of test-wiseness, poor item writing, or poor scoring. Once we are sure that those types of error have been eliminated, then items can be scored, aggregated scores created, and interpretations made about who needs to be taught what next.

Another important message is that objectively scored item formats take considerable work to create, but they are relatively easy to mark, while the reverse tends to be true of the types of tasks described in Chapters 3 and 4. Objectively scored question formats can elicit higher-order thinking skills, though this is very much a function of the question writer's imagination and skill. Nonetheless, the ability to ensure rapid and broad coverage of facts, details, and ideas is not a bad thing in itself, since higher-order thinking skills require competence with the objects being thought about. Hence, while the item formats in this chapter are most frequently used for summative purposes, they can effectively inform both teachers as to improvement priorities, provided the analysis of the items focuses on the aggregated constructs established in the test blueprint or template introduced at the start of the chapter.[34]

Answers to Test of Best Practice in Writing Multiple-Choice Questions

Answers:

1. (d) Grammatical cue; an requires Vowel
2. (c) Breaks syntactic pattern only singular
3. (b) Longest option
4. (a) Repeats key word; first option
5. (d) Grammatical cue; only Verb plural
6. (c) Only one word constant in all options
7. (b) Answer given elsewhere in test
8. (a) Fallows pattern of keys

Seven

Scores and Statistics

All tests use scores to report performance. Teachers can determine some of these scores for themselves using simple tools, but they need some familiarity with the technical tools used by test publishers to communicate essential information about test quality and student performance. This requires a brief primer on educational test statistics. Specifically, this chapter will address issues involved in determining test quality (i.e., psychometrics) and understanding a variety of scores used to describe performance.

SCORE CALCULATION

Different kinds of statistical models have been developed to calculate an ability or proficiency score depending on the type of scoring used. Scores are either dichotomous or they are a rating. Some tests have penalties for guessing that may discourage students from trying to answer items about which they are less than 100% certain. This approach is generally not useful in formative classroom contexts, where the goal is to encourage students to demonstrate what they do and do not know so that both teacher and student can work on those things that are not understood. In a high-stakes MCQ test for accountability or certification, the tendency to guess is better handled by scoring items using Item Response Theory (IRT)[147,148] which weights a total score by the difficulty of the items answered correctly without having to penalise guessing.

Dichotomous Score Calculation

Objectively scored items are normally scored dichotomously (i.e., the answer is either right = 1 or wrong = 0). This approach makes it easy to create a sum score or percentage score using classical test theory[145] which counts how many items a student got correct. It is worth noting that each score of 1 represents a categorical statement that the item has been answered correctly; the sum of the items correct is converted into a continuous variable that permits the calculation of test statistics (e.g., mean, standard deviation, and standard error of measurement, or SEM). These statistics allow a number of useful interpretations, including (a) whether the test was too hard or easy, or whether the class had been well taught or not, (b) whether score differences are within chance or not, and (c) the ability of a test-taker relative to others.

In contrast, modern test theory uses IRT,[146] a probabilistic statistical approach that determines both the difficulty of each item and the ability of each test-taker on the assumption that the probability of getting an item right increases with greater ability in a domain, but allows the possibility that weak students can get hard items right and vice versa. This method effectively looks past the number of items answered correctly to the difficulty of those items and weights the score accordingly. This means that unless students answer exactly the same items correctly, their scores will differ, not by how many they answer, but by the difficulty of the items. An important consequence of IRT is that it encourages teachers to give students the opportunity to answer hard questions and rewards students for answering challenging questions; the score cannot go up unless harder items are answered. This is quite a contrast from the classical test approach in which easy items give the same reward as hard items, generating the idea that improvement or growth is the ability to answer more questions correctly in an ever decreasing time. That model of learning and assessment produces students who develop maladaptive motivations and learning strategies when they are eventually exposed to harder and more challenging tasks.[149] Hence, it is good testing theory, as well as good learning and teaching psychology, to include increasingly difficult items in tests, so that students can be rewarded for answering correctly the harder questions and tasks.

Rating Scale Score Calculation

A challenge to score calculation occurs when tasks are rated across a multi-point scale for quality rather than simply for correctness. For example, university grades (i.e., A, B, C, D, and F, sometimes with + and − augmentation) comprise a multi-point scale, as do assignments or tasks scored out of values greater than 1 (e.g., 5, 20, or 100). A similar situation takes place when there are partial scores (e.g., 0 = wrong; 1 = correct procedures but wrong answer; 2 = right procedures and answer). These scores attempt to reflect an underlying continuum of quality from none to outstanding to which a certain number of marks or a letter grade is attached. This situation can be modelled statistically using IRT techniques such as partial credit modeling[150] or graded response modeling.[149] These techniques identify the probability that each score threshold (i.e., the point on the ability/difficulty scale at which the probability shifts from getting a lower to the next higher mark) exists in the intended order (e.g., the probability of getting a C is at a lower point on the difficulty scale than that of getting a B) and that there is a roughly equal range of abilities at which there is a good probability of getting each score. With these statistical insights it is possible to be confident that the raters are using the score points on the scale defensibly and plausibly.

Normally, objectively scored items are treated as if performance on any one item is uninfluenced by any other test-related factor (i.e., items are independent). However, many dichotomous questions are associated with a common stimulus material that provides information that has to be used in order to answer the item (e.g., a reading passage or set of data). If two or more questions are based around such common stimulus material, the items should be scored as a testlet (i.e., a mini-test) rather than as independent items. A testlet of two items then has potential scores of 0, 1, or 2, and analysis requires a statistical model that takes into account this lack of local independence.[150]

From the classroom teacher perspective, the sum of items answered correctly is extremely easy to use and will provide useful insights, especially if differences within the SEM are treated as being equivalent. However, standardised tests produced by test publishers, state accountability agencies, or international testing agencies will probably make use of IRT to more accurately account for item difficulty. Teachers do need to be aware of what statistical model is being used to score tests so that they can explain to students and their families how scores were created.

RELIABILITY

A major goal of test theory is to demonstrate that the scoring process has been consistent between markers or over a set of items. Establishing consistency in scoring processes means that the many threats to valid scoring identified in Chapter 3 have been overcome. One common way to do that is to determine the degree to which markers agree with each other using the standards described in Chapter 3. Tests that use MCQs or other objectively scored items are likely to report estimates for consistency reliability and item point biserial statistics, so users can have confidence in the demonstrated ability of the test to provide a robust estimate of a construct and an ordering of test-takers.

Reliability is founded on the classical test theory idea that an obtained or observed (O) score on a test is made up of the true ability of the test-taker plus error in the testing process (i.e., $O = \tau + e$).[151] Because the truth of a person's ability in an educational domain is latent (i.e., not directly observable), psychometrics approaches the problem of estimating the true score by calculating the size of the error component among a set of items in a test. To do this, degrees of similarity or overlap among items are calculated. These correlation coefficients are used subsequently to estimate the degree to which items intercorrelate (Cronbach's alpha[152]), the degree to which items correlate with the total score (point biserial), and the margin of error in an observed test score (the SEM). Correlations are constrained to be between -1.00 and $+1.00$, with values close to 1.00 indicating high degrees of similarity. Negative values mean that the two variables behave in an inverse fashion; for example, neurotic people tend to score low on emotional stability but high on reaction to stress. In a test situation, inverse correlations would indicate items are not eliciting responses consistent with the intended design of a test.

Items that correlate strongly with each other are likely to have some intrinsic characteristic in common. It is expected that items with the same content characteristics (e.g., grammar, algebra, photosynthesis) used to design a test (see Test Design in Chapter 6) will be more highly correlated than items of a different subscore. Items within an intended subscore ought to be positively correlated with each other. While multiple techniques for establishing the reliability of subscores are being validated,[153] techniques for establishing the reliability of total test scores are rather more well established[154] and it is expected these approaches or variations will become robust for test subscores.

The simplest metric reported is the estimate of consistency reliability, which is either based on the average inter-item correlation or the median of all split-half inter-item correlations (e.g., Cronbach's alpha[155]). Alpha is highly ubiquitous and will be usually reported by test developers despite its imperfections.[156] Alpha indicates the extent to which items covary; that is, test-takers who get many right are likely to do well on all items. Values greater than .70 are at a minimum for classroom testing, whereas high-stakes accountability or certification testing should have values greater than .90. Other procedures that could be used are confirmatory factor analytic approaches that have fit indices to show whether the item groups explain the test responses well[145] or IRT separation indices that show how well the test items are able to separate people according to their latent ability.[155]

Another statistic is the correlation of each item to the total score after removing the item from the total score (i.e., point biserial correlation r_{pb}). This statistic is appropriate when the total score is continuous (i.e., the sum of all items correct) and the item score is categorical (i.e., the item is right or wrong). The goal here is to determine whether scores for any item within a test order students in the same manner as the total score does. Many standardised tests select items that have $r_{pb} > .20$ values, although any positive value may support the use of the item.

Hence, with these simple correlations the consistency of scoring is established and the quality of items to discriminate in the same way as the test total score is established. These values permit estimation of the accuracy of an observed score.

Standard Error of Measurement (SEM)

Once the reliability of a score is established, it becomes possible to determine how accurate an observed score is. Accuracy is the other aspect of reliability, in that it focuses more on how truthful the observed score is. If tests were perfect and students had no recall of their previous answers and had no extra time to learn or be taught, their score should be identical between two different administrations of a test. However, since items do not perfectly correlate with each other and the total, and because it is impossible to impose these conditions on human test-takers, we are required to estimate a range of scores that would be most likely the next time the student is tested. This is akin to the notion of margin of error in opinion poll surveying which makes claims such as candidate X is favoured by 46% +/− 3%.

The SEM indicates the number of marks a score could vary by chance, without any substantive change in the student's ability.[155] SEM is calculated by multiplying the standard deviation of the test by the square root of 1 minus the test reliability estimate (SEM = SD × $\sqrt{(1 - \alpha)}$). Thus, a score of 76% on a test that has an SEM equal to 6% means that there is a 68% probability that the true score of this person falls in the 70–82% range; to reach 95% confidence, two SEM ranges need to used (i.e., 64–88%). In most schooling practices, one SEM is considered sufficient to analyse differences between students or between testing times. Using the SEM range means that if two candidates or tests fall with one SEM of each other, the difference is attributable to chance, not something real.

The SEM is a powerful tool for the teacher and test interpreter since it estimates the amount of uncertainty in a score. This discourages teachers, students, and parents from making a big deal about small differences and encourages realism around how hard it is to grow in learning. Getting higher scores on a test may be a matter of diligent practice, but developing real ability in a domain seems to be quite a different matter.

SCORE INTERPRETATION

Once test scores have been demonstrated to be consistently obtained and have an acceptable margin of error, the raw score may not be very useful. Raw scores without interpretive context tend to be ambiguous. A score of 83 may not be out of 100, the test may have been very easy, the amount of preparatory teaching and studying may have been inadequate, the average of the class may have been much higher, and so on. Hence, guidance is needed to understand a score.

Traditionally, standardised tests generate scores that provide a total score and sometimes a rank order; for example, traditional school testing in Hong Kong lists students by total percentage score and rank order in class or year group. As argued elsewhere,[34] these simplistic interpretations are problematic since the difficulty of the test is unknown and the reference group might not represent a normal ability population. Hence, without context and conventions for interpreting scores, a numeric value by itself is relatively meaningless.

There are three major comparisons that can aid in understanding a score:

1. How good is the score compared to similar people taking the test (*norm-referenced interpretation*)?

2. How good is the score compared to standards and objectives according to the curriculum or teaching plan (*criterion-referenced interpretation*)?
3. How good is the score compared to previous efforts (*ipsative-referenced interpretation*)?

Issues with ipsative-referenced scores were touched on in Chapter 5 in the Reporting section. This section deals with the strengths and weaknesses of norm-referenced and criterion-referenced types of score.

Norm-Referenced Comparisons

Of the three comparisons—norm-referenced, criterion-referenced, and ipsative-referenced—almost everyone understands comparison with other people. The person we most usefully compare ourselves with is usually not the best (e.g., not Tiger Woods in golf, Lewis Hamilton in F1 driving, nor Albert Einstein in physics) but rather the average. In published tests, the authors have developed a test with a representative group of learners similar to those who are intended to be evaluated with the test. That representative group's performance provides the comparison for interpreting a newly tested group of students' performance. This comparison group's performance is known as the 'norm' for the test. Note norm does not imply normal; it simply means typical or average for a certain population.

If new test-takers perform better than the norm, this is a pleasing result. However, there is no guarantee that the students did better than the norm because of high-quality teaching. Many schools do not enrol representative samples of the population, so there are advantages relative to the norm, if the tested group is drawn from the upper half of the socio-economic range. Conversely, if students score below the norm, this may not mean there has been poor quality teaching; there may have been real progress or value added, but which does not exceed the norm score. It is well established that schools with high numbers of minority students[157] or students from socio-economically deprived communities[158] tend to score lower than the norm, in part because the norm samples from the whole population, not just from students with these backgrounds. Thus, being lower or better than the norm is not an invitation to shame or pride in itself. Instead, schools need to investigate student strengths and weaknesses within the total score (helped if the test provides these curriculum-related subscores[34]) and identify priority needs that they can address. Indeed, systematic analysis of student achievement data can help teachers and school leaders identify effective levers for improving teaching and student outcomes.[11]

The usefulness of the norm is that it identifies not only whether the scores are lower or higher than the expected average, but also whether the difference is large enough to be concerned about. Scores that are within a standard error of the norm do not differ by more than chance. Scores that are within the SEM are highly likely to be the same as the norm at another test event. It is clear that the difference between first and 10th in a group will matter psychologically and, perhaps, even socially. However, if the scores are close together, then the difference in rank obscures the more important fact that the scores did not differ by much. Indeed, differences in the Olympics between first place and fourth place (out of the medals) are usually extremely small in terms of speed, distance, weight, skill, and so on. The rank matters but the actual difference in achievement might not. Educators need to pay attention to this and guide students and families into a proper understanding of scores.[159]

It is worth noting that most standardised tests do not use percentage correct as a way of indicating student performance. Instead, transformed scores or scale scores are used to communicate this information in an attempt to get away from the idea of percent correct. This is done using the normal or Gaussian distribution of scores (often known as the 'bell curve') to create a new midpoint score and standard deviation. The normal curve is shaped this way because in variables for which a large number of measurements exist, the scores will cluster close to the mean. For example, if chocolate bars are meant to be 100 grams, the actual mean score will probably be close to but slightly over 100 grams to ensure that almost all bars will be at least to the published value. In a sample of 1,000 chocolate bars taken off a production line, it is unlikely they will all be exactly the same weight due to minor variations in the process. Assume the mean weight is 101.5 grams and that the standard deviation is only 0.5 grams. This means that 500 bars will be close to but below the mean of 101.5 and that only 0.1% (1 in 1,000) will be less than 100 grams (i.e., be more than three standard deviations below the mean).

This property of large numbers can be used to create other scores by mathematically transforming the mean and standard deviation values to generate a score system that might communicate the relative rank of people who took the test relative to the norming group. Hence, the transformed norm-referenced score indicates not how many questions a person got right or how hard the questions were that were answered correctly, although this will be correlated with the score. Rather the score indicates where in the distribution the performance lies. Nonetheless, it is educationally useful to know how well someone has performed compared with other similar people. Teaching responses probably should be different if a score is substantially below, at, or above the average. Customised or personalised teaching, activities, or materials in response to substantially different performance on standardised assessments is considered by many to be an appropriate response that aligns curriculum and teaching with identified student needs and abilities.[160]

A number of transformed scores exist in education:

Percentile. The most basic rank-order score is the percentile (%ile), which is a number between 1 and 100 that indicates where a specific score sits in the distribution of the norm group scores. If the mean of a test is 55, then a person with 55 has a %ile score of 50th, while a person at the second standard deviation above the mean would have %ile of 97.5, indicating that only 2.5% of the sample got better scores. A useful %ile is the median (i.e., the score at the middle of the distribution). The median is less sensitive to large extreme values than the average, so when evaluating incomes or house prices the average will give a much larger number than the median, if a few very rich or expensive houses are in the sample. Thus, %iles indicate clearly where in a distribution a person's score lies. However, it takes much less of a score change to move from the 40th %ile to the 50th %ile than move the same distance at either tail of the distribution. This means that moving 10 %iles is harder work at the bottom and top of the rank order than it is in the middle. Given that scores have error, for students in the middle of the distribution a change in score that could be random might have a large and misleading impact on %ile score. Given this variability in the meaning of a %ile, %iles cannot be averaged across subjects;

instead special non-parametric statistics are needed.[62] While relatively intuitive, this type of scale is not recommended in analysing or reporting performance to school leaders, parents, or students.

Stanine. The stanine (standardised nine) score solves some of these problems by dividing the 100 %iles into nine equally sized blocks, each of which covers half of a standard deviation. The middle score (Stanine 5) covers the half standard deviation surrounding the mean (i.e., M +/− .25 SD). Each subsequent stanine either side of Stanine 5 covers another ½ standard deviation. Because of the normal distribution property, 55% of all candidates will get Stanine 4, 5, or 6—these are the average group. The lowest performing candidates (that is those below the 23rd %ile) will get Stanines 1 to 3, while the highest performing 22.50% will get Stanines 7 to 9. Instead of having each rank represent a different amount of raw score, each stanine represents the same amount of raw score (.50 SD)—and thus, stanines can be mathematically manipulated. This means that looking at a profile of performance across multiple subjects with the stanine is feasible. Another advantage is that they account better for SEM because a stanine is larger than the SEM. However, this means it is also harder to determine whether improvement is happening since the stanine is so coarse; changes of two stanines are needed to be sure a change is happening.

Normal Curve Equivalent (NCE). The NCE is a hybrid between the %ile and stanine in that it creates an equal interval scale like the stanine but spread over a 1–100 scale (mean = 50, SD = 21.06) like the %ile.[161] Being spread out over a longer scale than the stanine, the NCE is more sensitive to change, but like the stanine, comparisons over time and tests are possible.

Standard or scale scores. Any of the normal curve scores can be transformed to an arbitrarily selected mean and standard deviation (i.e., a standard or scale score[161]). For example, the intelligence quotient (IQ) score has a mean of 100 no matter how many items were involved in the test. The standard deviation is 15, meaning that approximately 68% of participants get a score within one standard deviation of the mean; in this case between 85 and 115. Only 2.50% of people will get a score greater than 130 or less than 70; so be sceptical of claims that a person's IQ is over 145. Many standardised tests will set the mean at a reasonably high number (e.g., 500 or 1,000) and impose a large standard deviation (e.g., 50 or 100). This approach helps reduce the notion that the score indicates what percent of items were answered correctly and allows the extension of the scale to cater for much weaker performing candidates without going below zero.

Grade or age equivalent scores. These transform performance relative to the norm performance of students in the same grade or age as the test-taker. A student who performs at the average for their grade or age will have a grade or age equivalent score equal to their actual grade or age.[161] An exceptionally good student may be performing at the same level as students two grades or years older, in which case their score will be current age or grade plus 2. An advantage of this scale is that it speaks a natural language: 'my Grade 2 child is reading at Grade 4 level.' This equivalent system requires having well-established values for performance at each grade level and presupposes that the content being tested is vertically aligned across grades. If content areas vary markedly across grades, the grade equivalent notion becomes suspect since apples are not being compared with apples, though this should be less problematic with the introduction of the US Common Core State Standards Initiative.[162]

Criterion-Referenced Scores

Criterion-referenced scores attempt to describe performance relative to objective standards for a learning outcome domain.[163] These are most useful in industry or vocational education where quality indicators for skills or knowledge are readily established. Standards for many job skills specify such aspects as speed and accuracy in being able to perform the task. For example, before the introduction of computer-based keyboarding, a minimum entry standard for a beginning typist was 35 words per minute with no more than one error per minute. These standards function as benchmarks towards which students are taught and against which their performance can be assessed. With these criteria and observed student performance relative to them, formative educational planning becomes feasible to address any needs that are identified. In this framework it is possible for all students to meet the intended learning outcomes specified in the criteria—an educational goal with laudable intention. Teaching that aims for all students to succeed at fulfilling minimum criteria in literacy, numeracy, or job readiness, and so on is a desired goal in most societies. Thus, giving students rank scores is pointless when the decision is dichotomous (met or not met the criteria).

An advantage for criterion-referenced approaches is that when a learning domain is explicitly observable and agreed minimum competency is easy to describe, this approach is very accurate. However, in complex cognitive domains when there is much subjectivity in discovering indicators of performance or in agreeing upon competency standards, this approach is problematic.[164] The procedures described in Chapter 3 need to be brought into play when evaluating whether students have met various levels or standards of performance relative to criterial statements in complex domains. Indeed, the art of grading described in Chapter 5 is also a form of judgement rating based on criteria.

The real challenge in criterion-referenced assessment is in defining the standards by which performances will be evaluated. It is possible to work backwards from a body of student work to determine what appropriate standards or criteria can be used to describe quality levels in even quite complex domains. This process is called 'standard setting' and involves selecting rank-ordered student work and determining the implicit characteristics lying underneath the decision to rank the work where it is in the continuum. Multiple standard-setting procedures exist[165] and each approach has its own strengths. Here are two examples:

- **Test difficulty.** Teachers are asked to judge the difficulty of tasks on a test given the expected level of learning (e.g., grade or stream/track). On a very difficult test, assessors could agree that a score of 30% represents the minimum level of competency for a C, in which case all students who obtained 30% are then given the official score for minimal competency (e.g., 50%). In contrast, students who got 60% on test deemed to be too easy may have just exhibited minimal competency, and their scores should be reported as 50%.
- **Rank order.** Order student work from best to worst based on a holistic judgment. Then determine the qualities of performance demonstrated by the best, middle, and lowest performing students in a domain. More systematically, raters could be asked to describe characteristics that all top-half work has but which none of the bottom-half work has. This empirical binary boundary[166] process could continue for all the required grade boundaries. From rank-ordered

material, it is possible to derive indicators that are associated with standards of performance which also happen to be located at certain places in the rank order. In other words, underneath each criterion might just lie a norm.[167]

Whatever the nature of criteria, they function most powerfully to inform teachers and students as to important aspects of learning that have to be evident in student work and in the scaffolding that teachers provide in the classroom. It is this aspect that makes criterion-referenced assessment superior to norm-referenced testing. It may not be easy to raise a student's rank-order position, especially in a 'rising tide' environment in which all students are improving. However, it ought to be possible to raise student performance in terms of agreed standards and criteria about the intended characteristics of learning goals or objectives. Since the dominant purpose of assessment is to inform educational responses to student learning needs, it is fairly clear that notwithstanding the advanced technical information available in norm-referenced comparison scores, the real goal of assessment and teaching is helping more and more students develop the desired skills and abilities as specified in learning objectives or outcomes. For that, criterion-referenced assessment of some sort is needed.

Glossary

Assessment — A general process of collecting information (e.g., tests, observations, question and answer, etc.) to describe the characteristics (e.g., strengths or weaknesses) of a product, process, or person. Often treated as synonymous with **evaluation**, though often without **formative** or value implications

Authentic assessment — Assessment type that attempts to mimic real-world activities. Requires learner to demonstrate, perhaps in a simulated environment, skills similar to those used outside a classroom context.

Classical test theory — A statistical approach to analysing tests based on the assumption that the sum of all items answered correctly is the best estimate of ability. Focus is on estimating the error component—the **standard error of measurement (SEM)**—in a test score so as to lead to appropriate decisions and actions.

Conceptions — Belief systems, usually arising implicitly from experiences with a phenomenon, that guide persons in responding to or understanding the phenomenon.

Constructed response — Test items or tasks that require the test-taker to create their own answer rather than selecting or choosing from a set of possible answers.

Correlation A statistical measure of linear association between variables, ranging from -1.00 to $+1.00$, with positive values indicating that both variables increase simultaneously, while negative values mean that the variables go in opposite directions.

Criterion-referenced A score or task that is aligned to and interpreted by reference to explicit statements as to what the assessee can do.

Cronbach's alpha The median of all inter-item **correlations** used to indicate the degree to which a set of items correlate or belong to the same pool or group. Values at least $\alpha > .70$ are required to indicate that items form a coherent group.

Dichotomous A score system in which only two conditions are possible (e.g., right vs. wrong). Items normally scored $0 =$ wrong or not answered, $1 =$ correct.

Discrimination The parameter that captures the tendency of high scoring test-takers to get an item right more than lower-scoring test-takers. In **CTT** this is expressed most often as the **point biserial** correlation. In **IRT** this is expressed as 'a', representing the angle of the item characteristic curve slope at the item difficulty point.

E-portfolio An electronic or digital **portfolio** method of assembling learning objects and activities for selection, dissemination, or display.

Essay Academic writing task that requires students to engage in a cognitive task in

Glossary

	relation to a certain set of content. In examinations, performance is normally timed and the task may not have been pre-specified.
Evaluation	A process of determining the value, merit, or worth of a product, process, or person.
Exemplar	A piece of work that has been highlighted to show its strengths and deficiencies and explains why it has been graded in a specific way.
Feedback	Feedback is information to the user (teacher or learner) that describes characteristics of the work or process and provides directions as to how further improvement by either the instructor or student can be achieved.
Formative	Any data collection or decision making taken early enough to support improvements in a product, person, or process.
Grading	The act of assigning a letter grade to student work that best reflects the quality and merit of the work.
Ipsative-referenced	Comparison of work to previous performances of the individual who did the work. Commonly used by athletes to track their progress to a Personal Best.
Item difficulty	How hard a test question is. In **CTT** this is the proportion of people who get it right. In **IRT** it is the ability point (b) on the ability/difficulty dimension (θ) where test-takers have a 50% probability of getting the item correct.
Item Response Theory (IRT)	A probabilistic statistical scoring model, using the log odds, that defines a person's ability by the difficulty of all items

answered correctly. Up to three different parameters can be used to describe a test item's characteristics (i.e., **item difficulty, discrimination**, and **pseudo-chance**). Selection of IRT model depends on assumptions made about the measurement of ability.

Judgment of Learning A self-prediction of how well a learner will do on a forthcoming test after having studied for the test material. This is a type of **self-assessment**.

Judgment-scored The process of judging or rating the quality of work instead of marking. Often requires matching work against standards expressed in **rubrics** or **grading** instructions.

Marking The process of determining whether an answer was correct. Sometimes called *scoring*.

Multiple choice) questions (MCQ A form of selected response tasks in which students select the best or correct answer from a set of plausible options.

Mean The mathematical average of a set of data points or scores.

Median The midpoint or 50th percentile of a distribution of scores.

Norm The distribution of scores of a representative sample of test-takers against whom new test-takers can be evaluated.

Normal curve equivalent (NCE) A transformed score based on the Gaussian normal distribution in which a 100 point equal interval scale has a **mean** = 50 and a **SD** = 21.06.

Norm-referenced A scoring system which compares new test-taker performance against the performance of the **norm** or some other reference group. This positions a person relative to other test-takers.

Objectively scored Tasks for which there is an agreed single correct answer and which potentially could be machine scored. These include **multiple choice questions (MCQ)**.

Peer assessment The appraisal of student work by fellow learners, usually with the goal of generating **feedback** as to the quality characteristics and directions for improvement. Can include peer **marking**.

Percentage Proportion of items out of a maximum of 100 answered correctly.

Percentile Rank-order position relative to the **norm** or other reference group expressed as a value between 1–100. Each number expresses the **percentage** of the comparison group who got scores lower than the test-taker.

Point biserial A **correlation** value between an item and the total score, after the item being considered has been removed from the total score. This expresses the **discrimination** of an item in **CTT**.

Portfolio A collection of learning objects or activities that can be used to display work quality and/or processes.

Pseudo-chance The parameter that captures the probability of test-takers with extremely low ability on θ getting an item right, despite having close to no ability measured by the test item.

Rank order The general class of scores indicating position relative to a reference group or

	norm. Position may not reflect large differences in actual score.
Rating	The process of judging the quality or merit of work and assigning values making use of an agreed **rating scale**.
Rating scale	The range of agreed scores, marks, or grades which reflect criteria or **standards** by which work should be evaluated. Can include analytic or holistic **rubrics**.
Reliability	A property of scores and scoring or rating processes. Reliability refers to both the consistency of scoring or **marking** processes (e.g., between markers or performances at different times) and the accuracy or truthfulness of a mark or grade in representing a test-taker's ability. In **CTT**, a reliable test has a low **standard error of measurement (SEM)**. In **IRT**, a reliable test provides a high degree of separation between test-takers.
Rubric	A structured **rating scale** which provides information as to the qualities or characteristics of ordered levels, standards, or grades against which a performance or product is evaluated. Holistic rubrics capture all important aspects or features of the work into an overall classification. Analytic rubrics specify various dimensions or components that are evaluated separately.
Selected response	A test question format in which the student chooses from among possible options. Includes **multiple choice questions (MCQ)** and other formats that are **objectively scored**.

Glossary

Self-assessment — A process in which a student describes the quality and/or evaluates the merit of their own work products or processes. May be guided by a **rubric**.

Standard — A statement of the qualities of work products or processes which are expected by an assessor, employer, or teacher. Often associated with use of **rating scales** or **rubrics** for **grading** purposes.

Standard deviation (SD) — A measure of spread around the **mean** within a set of scores. Quantifies the dispersion of scores around the **mean**.

Standard error of measurement (SEM) — As used in **CTT**, the SEM is the range of scores that an observed score could vary by chance, without any substantive change in the student's ability. SEM is calculated by multiplying the **standard deviation (SD)** of the test by the square root of 1 minus the test **reliability** estimate.

Standardised test — A test which has been designed to be administered and scored according to specified rules. Usually relies on **selected response** items and generates **norm-referenced** scores to aid interpretation.

Standard setting — A process by which the range of **scores** or **marks** is converted into **grades** or levels that express desired quality **standards**.

Stanine — A transformed score of nine points, each equivalent to ½ a **standard deviation (SD)** that indicates the **rank-order** position of a person's score relative to a relevant **norm**. Values 1–3 are considered low, 4–6 are medium, and 7–9 are high.

Subscore — A component score within a test that captures the common construct shared by

	the items within the overall domain. For example, a reading comprehension test may have subscores for vocabulary and grammar.
Summative	Any data collection or decision making taken after further changes can no longer be implemented and used to evaluate the characteristics and/or merit and worth of a product, person, or process.
Test	Any method of or procedure for obtaining information about the quality, presence, or amount of test-taker knowledge or skill within a domain. Often synonymous with **assessment**.
Test difficulty	The overall difficulty of a test. Can be ascertained by reference to the **mean** or **standards** for which the test was designed.
Total score	In **CTT**, the sum of all items in a test answered correctly, commonly expressed as a **percentage**. In **IRT**, the ability estimate derived from the chosen formula.
Traffic lights	A **self-assessment** process in which students indicate the quality of their understanding using red ('stop, I don't understand'), yellow ('proceed with caution, I'm not 100% sure I understand'), and green ('proceed, I understand this') colours. Often displayed publically to the teacher in a classroom setting.
Validity	A judgment and argument, based on theory and empirical evidence, as to the appropriateness or defensibility of any interpretation or actions arising from an assessment or test process. All aspects of assessment design, administration, scoring,

feedback, and reporting fall under the auspices of validity.

Value-added measures A statistical approach to determining the impact or effect of a programme, teacher, or school by taking into account the different starting levels.

For further reference, an extensive glossary of assessment and measurement terms published by the National Council on Measurement in Education can be found online.[168]

References

1. Ecclestone, K., & Pryor, J. (2003). 'Learning careers' or 'assessment careers'? The impact of assessment systems on learning. *British Educational Research Journal*, 29(4), 471–488.
2. Brown, G. T. L. (2008). *Conceptions of assessment: Understanding what assessment means to teachers and students*. New York: Nova Science Publishers.
3. Deneen, C. C., & Brown, G. T. L. (2016). The impact of conceptions of assessment on assessment literacy in a teacher education program. *Cogent Education*, 3, 1225380. doi:10.1080/2331186X.2016.1225380
4. Ajzen, I. (1991). The theory of planned behavior. *Organizational Behavior and Human Decision Processes*, 50, 179–211.
5. Newton, P. E. (2007). Clarifying the purposes of educational assessment. *Assessment in Education: Principles, Policy & Practice*, 14(2), 149–170.
6. Shohamy, E. (2001). *The power of tests: A critical perspective on the uses of language tests*. Harlow, UK: Pearson Education.
7. Brown, G. T. L. (2004). Teachers' conceptions of assessment: Implications for policy and professional development. *Assessment in Education: Principles, Policy & Practice*, 11(3), 301–318. doi:10.1080/0969594042000304609
8. Crooks, T. J. (2010). Classroom assessment in policy context (New Zealand). In B. McGraw, P. Peterson, & E. L. Baker (Eds.), *The international encyclopedia of education* (3rd ed., pp. 443–448). Oxford, UK: Elsevier.
9. Brown, G. T. L. (2011). Teachers' conceptions of assessment: Comparing primary and secondary teachers in New Zealand. *Assessment Matters*, 3, 45–70.
10. Brown, G. T. L., Harris, L. R., & Harnett, J. (2012). Teacher beliefs about feedback within an assessment for learning environment: Endorsement of improved learning over student well-being. *Teaching and Teacher Education*, 28(7), 968–978. doi:10.1016/j.tate.2012.05.003

References

11 Lai, M. K., & Schildkamp, K. (2016). In-service teacher professional learning: Use of assessment in data-based decision-making. In G. T. L. Brown, & L. R. Harris (Eds.), *Handbook of human and social conditions in assessment* (pp. 77–94). New York: Routledge.

12 Nichols, S. L., & Harris, L. R. (2016). Accountability assessment's effects on teachers and schools. In G. T. L. Brown, & L. R. Harris (Eds.), *Handbook of human and social conditions in assessment* (pp. 40–56). New York: Routledge.

13 Hofstede, G. (2007). A European in Asia. *Asian Journal of Social Psychology*, 10(1), 16–21. doi:10.1111/j.1467-839X.2006.00206.x

14 Brown, G. T. L., & Gao, L. (2015). Chinese teachers' conceptions of assessment for and of learning: Six competing and complementary purposes. *Cogent Education*, 2(1), 993836. doi:10.1080/2331186X.2014.993836

15 Kennedy, K. J. (2016). Exploring the influence of culture on assessment: The case of teachers' conceptions of assessment in confucian-heritage cultures. In G. T. L. Brown, & L. R. Harris (Eds.), *Handbook of human and social conditions in assessment* (pp. 404–419). New York: Routledge.

16 Fives, H., & Buehl, M. M. (2012). Spring cleaning for the 'messy' construct of teachers' beliefs: What are they? Which have been examined? What can they tell us? In K. R. Harris, S. Graham, & T. Urdan (Eds.), *APA educational psychology handbook: Individual differences and cultural and contextual factors* (Vol. 2, pp. 471–499). Washington, DC: APA.

17 Bonner, S. M. (2016). Teachers' perceptions about assessment: Competing narratives. In G. T. L. Brown, & L. R. Harris (Eds.), *Handbook of human and social conditions in assessment* (pp. 21–39). New York: Routledge.

18 Brown, G. T. L. (2016). Improvement and accountability functions of assessment: Impact on teachers' thinking and action. In A. M. Peters (Ed.), *Encyclopedia of educational philosophy and theory* (pp. 1–6). Singapore: Springer Singapore.

19 Brown, G. T. L., & Hirschfeld, G. H. F. (2008). Students' conceptions of assessment: Links to outcomes. *Assessment in Education: Principles, Policy & Practice*, 15(1), 3–17. doi:10.1080/09695940701876003

20 Brown, G. T. L., Peterson, E. R., & Irving, S. E. (2009). Beliefs that make a difference: Adaptive and maladaptive self-regulation in students' conceptions of assessment. In D. M. McInerney, G. T. L. Brown,

& G. A. D. Liem (Eds.), *Student perspectives on assessment: What students can tell us about assessment for learning* (pp. 159–186). Charlotte, NC, US: Information Age Publishing.

21 Wise, S. L., & Smith, L. F. (2016). The validity of assessment when students don't give good effort. In G. T. L. Brown, & L. R. Harris (Eds.), *Handbook of human and social conditions in assessment* (pp. 204–220). New York: Routledge.

22 Vogl, E., & Pekrun, R. (2016). Emotions that matter to achievement: Student feelings about assessment. In G. T. L. Brown, & L. R. Harris (Eds.), *Handbook of human and social conditions in assessment* (pp. 111–128). New York: Routledge.

23 Dinsmore, D. L., & Wilson, H. E. (2016). Student participation in assessment: Does it influence self-regulation? In G. T. L. Brown, & L. R. Harris (Eds.), *Handbook of human and social factors in assessment* (pp. 145–168). New York: Routledge.

24 Murdock, T. B., Stephens, J. M., & Groteweil, M. M. (2016). Student dishonesty in the face of assessment: Who, why, and what we can do about it. In G. T. L. Brown, & L. R. Harris (Eds.), *Handbook of human and social conditions in assessment* (pp. 186–203). New York: Routledge.

25 McMillan, J. H. (2016). Section discussion: Student perceptions of assessment. In G. T. L. Brown, & L. R. Harris (Eds.), *Handbook of human and social conditions in assessment* (pp. 221–243). New York: Routledge.

26 Brown, G. T. L. (2011). Self-regulation of assessment beliefs and attitudes: A review of the students' Conceptions of Assessment inventory. *Educational Psychology*, 31(6), 731–748. doi:10.1080/01443410.2011.599836

27 Messick, S. (1989). Validity. In R. L. Linn (Ed.), *Educational measurement* (3rd ed., pp. 13–103). Old Tappan, NJ: MacMillan.

28 Popham, W. J. (2000). *Modern educational measurement: Practical guidelines for educational leaders* (6th ed.). Boston: Allyn & Bacon.

29 Black, P., & Wiliam, D. (1998). Assessment and classroom learning. *Assessment in Education: Principles, Policy & Practice*, 5(1), 7–74.

30 Crooks, T. J. (1988). The impact of classroom evaluation practices on students. *Review of Educational Research*, 58(4), 438–481.

31 National Research Council. (2002). *Scientific research in education.* Washington, DC: National Academy Press.

32 Torrance, H., & Pryor, J. (1998). *Investigating formative assessment: Teaching, learning and assessment in the classroom.* Buckingham, UK: Open University Press.

References

33 Hattie, J. (2009). *Visible learning: A synthesis of meta-analyses in education.* London: Routledge.

34 Brown, G. T. L., & Hattie, J. A. (2012). The benefits of regular standardized assessment in childhood education: Guiding improved instruction and learning. In S. Suggate, & E. Reese (Eds.), *Contemporary debates in child development and education* (pp. 287–292). London: Routledge.

35 Xu, Y., & Brown, G. T. L. (2016). Teacher assessment literacy in practice: A reconceptualization. *Teaching and Teacher Education, 58,* 149–162. doi:10.1016/j.tate.2016.05.010

36 Moon, T. R. (2016). Differentiated instruction and assessment: An approach to classroom assessment in conditions of student diversity. In G. T. L. Brown, & L. R. Harris (Eds.), *Handbook of human and social conditions in assessment* (pp. 284–301). New York: Routledge.

37 Harris, L. R., & Brown, G. T. L. (2013). Opportunities and obstacles to consider when using peer- and self-assessment to improve student learning: Case studies into teachers' implementation. *Teaching and Teacher Education, 36,* 101–111. doi:10.1016/j.tate.2013.07.008

38 Peterson, E. R., & Irving, S. E. (2008). Secondary school students' conceptions of assessment and feedback. *Learning and Instruction, 18*(3), 238–250.

39 Meyer, L. H., McClure, J., Walkey, F., Weir, K. F., & McKenzie, L. (2009). Secondary student motivation orientations and standards-based achievement outcomes. *British Journal of Educational Psychology, 79*(2), 273–293. doi:10.1348/000709908X354591

40 Crooks, T. J., Kane, M. T., & Cohen, A. S. (1996). Threats to the valid use of assessments. *Assessment in Education: Principles, Policy & Practice, 3*(3), 265–285.

41 Alder, K. (2002). *The measure of all things: The seven-year odyssey that transformed the world.* London: Abacus.

42 AFT (American Federation of Teachers), NCME (National Council on Measurement in Education), & NEA (National Education Association). (1990). Standards for teacher competence in educational assessment of students. *Educational Measurement: Issues and Practice, 9*(4), 30–32.

43 AERA (American Educational Research Association), APA (American Psychological Association), & NCME (National Council for Measurement in Education). (2014). *The standards for educational & psychological testing.* Washington, DC: American Educational Research Association.

44 JCSEE (Joint Committee on Standards for Education Evaluation). (2015). *Classroom assessment standards for PreK–12 teachers*. [Kindle version]. Retrieved from www.amazon.com/Classroom-Assessment-Standards-PreK-12-Teachers-ebook/dp/B00V6C9RVO.

45 Keegan, P. J., Brown, G. T. L., & Hattie, J. A. C. (2013). A psychometric view of sociocultural factors in test validity: The development of standardised test materials for Māori medium schools in New Zealand/Aotearoa. In S. Phillipson, K. Ku, & S. N. Phillipson (Eds.), *Constructing educational achievement: A sociocultural perspective* (pp. 42–54). London: Routledge.

46 Brown, G. T. L. (2013). Assessing assessment for learning: Reconsidering the policy and practice. In M. East, & S. May (Eds.), *Making a difference in education and social policy* (pp. 121–137). Auckland, NZ: Pearson.

47 Sadler, D. R. (1989). Formative assessment and the design of instructional systems. *Instructional Science*, 18(2), 119–144. doi:10.1007/BF00117714

48 Scriven, M. (1991). Beyond formative and summative evaluation. In M. W. McLaughlin, & D. C. Phillips (Eds.), *Evaluation and education: At quarter century* (Vol. 90, Part II, pp. 19–64). Chicago, IL: NSSE.

49 Weeden, P., Winter, J., & Broadfoot, P. (2002). *Assessment: What's in it for schools?* London: RoutledgeFalmer.

50 Black, P. J. (1998). *Testing: Friend or foe? Theory and practice of assessment and testing*. London: Falmer Press.

51 Brookhart, S. M., & Nitko, A. J. (2008). *Assessment and grading in classrooms*. Upper Saddle River, NJ: Pearson Merrill Prentice Hall.

52 Pajares, M. F., & Graham, L. (1998). Formalist thinking and language arts instruction: Teachers' and students' beliefs about truth and caring in the teaching conversation. *Teaching and Teacher Education*, 14(8), 855–870.

53 Stemler, S. E. (2004). A comparison of consensus, consistency, and measurement approaches to estimating interrater reliability. *Practical Assessment, Research & Evaluation*, 9(4). Retrieved from http://tinyurl.com/m7grwph.

54 Brown, G. T. L., Glasswell, K., & Harland, D. (2004). Accuracy in the scoring of writing: Studies of reliability and validity using a New Zealand writing assessment system. *Assessing Writing*, 9(2), 105–121. doi:10.1016/j.asw.2004.07.001

References

55 Bloxham, S. (2009). Marking and moderation in the UK: False assumptions and wasted resources. *Assessment & Evaluation in Higher Education, 34*(2), 209–220.

56 Brown, G. T. L. (2009). The reliability of essay scores: The necessity of rubrics and moderation. In L. H. Meyer, S. Davidson, H. Anderson, R. Fletcher, P. M. Johnston, & M. Rees (Eds.), *Tertiary assessment and higher education student outcomes: Policy, practice and research* (pp. 40–48). Wellington, NZ: Ako Aotearoa.

57 Meadows, M., & Billington, L. (2005). *A review of the literature on marking reliability* (Report to the National Assessment Agency). London: AQA.

58 Brown, G. T. L. (2010). The validity of examination essays in higher education: Issues and responses. *Higher Education Quarterly, 64*(3), 276–291. doi:10.1111/j.1468-2273.2010.00460.x

59 Katz, I. R., & Gorin, J. S. (2016). Computerising assessment: Impacts on education stakeholders. In G. T. L. Brown, & L. R. Harris (Eds.), *Handbook of human and social conditions in assessment* (pp. 472–489). New York: Routledge.

60 Brennan, R. L., & Johnson, E. G. (1995). Generalizability of performance assessments. *Educational Measurement: Issues and Practice, 14*(4), 9–12, 27.

61 Brennan, R. L. (1996). Generalizability of performance assessments. In G. W. Phillips (Ed.), *Technical issues in large-scale performance assessment* (NCES 96-802) (pp. 19–58). Washington, DC: National Center for Education Statistics.

62 Linn, R. (1993). *Educational assessment: Expanded expectations and challenges* (CSE Tech. Rep. No. 351). Los Angeles, CA: University of California Los Angeles, National Center for Research on Evaluation, Standards, and Student Testing.

63 Linn, R. L., & Gronlund, N. E. (2000). *Measurement and assessment in teaching* (8th ed.). Upper Saddle River, NJ: Merrill/Prentice Hall.

64 Page, E. B. (1968). The use of the computer in analyzing student essays. *International Review of Education, 14*(2), 210–225.

65 Pollitt, A. (2012). Comparative judgement for assessment. *International Journal of Technology and Design Education, 22*(2), 157–170. doi:10.1007/s10798-011-9189-x

66 Shavelson, R. J., Ruiz-Primo, M. A., & Wiley, E. W. (2005). Windows into the mind. *Higher Education, 49*, 413–430.

References

67 Danielson, C., & Abrutyn, L. (1997). *An introduction to using portfolios in the classroom*. Alexandria, VA: Association for Supervision and Curriculum Development.

68 Kingore, B. (1993). *Portfolios: Enriching and assessing all students*. Des Moines: Leadership Publishers Inc.

69 Stefani, L., Mason, R., & Pegler, C. (2007). *The educational potential of e-portfolios: Supporting personal development and reflective learning*. London: Routledge.

70 Deneen, C. C., & Brown, G. T. L. (2013, April). *Understanding eportfolios as assessment in higher education*. Paper presented at the annual AERA conference, San Francisco, CA.

71 Deneen, C. C., Brown, G. T. L., & Carless, D. (2017). Students' conceptions of eportfolios as assessment and technology. *Innovations in Education and Teaching International*. Advanced online publication. doi:10.1080/14703297.2017.1281752

72 San Jose, D. L. (2016). Evaluating, Comparing, and Best Practice in Electronic Portfolio System Use. *Journal of Educational Technology Systems* (Advanced online publication) doi:10.1177/0047239516672049

73 Struyven, K., Dochy, F., & Janssens, S. (2008). The effects of hands-on experience on students' preferences for assessment methods. *Journal of Teacher Education*, 59(1), 69-88. doi:10.1177/0022487107311335

74 Struyven, K., Dochy, F., Janssens, S., Schelfhout, W., & Gielen, S. (2006). The overall effects of end-of-course assessment on student performance: A comparison between multiple choice testing, peer assessment, case-based assessment and portfolio assessment. *Studies in Educational Evaluation*, 32, 202–222.

75 Struyven, K., Blieck, Y., & De Roeck, V. (2014). The electronic portfolio as a tool to develop and assess pre-service student teaching competences: Challenges for quality. *Studies in Educational Evaluation*, 43, 40–54.

76 Struyven, K., & Devesa, J. (2016). Students' perceptions of novel forms of assessment. In G. T. L. Brown, & L. R. Harris (Eds.), *Handbook of human and social conditions in assessment* (pp. 129–144). New York: Routledge.

77 Myford, C. M., & Mislevy, R. J. (1995). *Monitoring and improving a portfolio assessment system* (MS 94–05). Princeton, NJ: Educational Testing Service.

References

78 Bryant, S. L., & Timmins, A. A. (2001). *Portfolio assessment: Instructional guide*. Hong Kong: Hong Kong Institute of Education.

79 Brown, G. T. L. (1999). Information literacy curriculum and assessment: Implications for schools from New Zealand. In J. Henri, & K. Bonanno (Eds.), *The information literate school community: Best practice* (pp. 55–74). Wagga Wagga: Charles Sturt University, Centre for Information Studies.

80 McKenzie, J. (2006). The no time slam dunk digital lesson. *The Question Mark*, 2(3). Retrieved from http://questioning.org/jan06/notime.html.

81 Linn, R., Baker, E., & Dunbar, S. (1991). Complex, performance-based assessment: Expectations and validation criteria. *Educational Researcher*, 20(8), 15–21.

82 Swaffield, S. (2011). Getting to the heart of authentic assessment for learning. *Assessment in Education: Principles, Policy & Practice*, 18(4), 433–449. doi:10.1080/0969594X.2011.582838

83 Newmann, F. M., Marks, H. M., & Gamoran, A. (1996). Authentic pedagogy and student performance. *American Journal of Education*, 104, 280–312.

84 Cowie, B. (2009). My teacher and my friends helped me learn: Student perceptions and experiences of classroom assessment. In D. M. McInerney, G. T. L. Brown, & G. A. D. Liem (Eds.), *Student perspectives on assessment: What students can tell us about assessment for learning* (pp. 85–105). Charlotte, NC: Information Age Publishing.

85 Brown, G. T. L., & Harris, L. R. (2013). Student self-assessment. In J. H. McMillan (Ed.), *The SAGE handbook of research on classroom assessment* (pp. 367–393). Thousand Oaks, CA: Sage.

86 Ross, J. A. (2006). The reliability, validity, and utility of self-assessment. *Practical Assessment Research & Evaluation*, 11(10). Retrieved from http://pareonline.net/getvn.asp?v=11&n=10.

87 Brown, G. T. L., Andrade, H., & Chen, F. (2015). Accuracy in student self-assessment: Directions and cautions for research. *Assessment in Education: Principles, Policy & Practice*, 22(4), 444–457. doi:10.1080/0969594X.2014.996523

88 Panadero, E., Brown, G. L., & Strijbos, J.-W. (2015). The future of student self-assessment: A review of known unknowns and potential directions. *Educational Psychology Review*, 28(4), 803–830. doi:10.1007/s10648-015-9350-2

References 143

89 Andrade, H. L., & Brown, G. T. L. (2016). Student self-assessment in the classroom. In G. T. L. Brown, & L. R. Harris (Eds.), *Handbook of human and social conditions in assessment* (pp. 319–334). New York: Routledge.

90 Butler, R. (2011). Are positive illusions about academic competence always adaptive, under all circumstances? New results and future directions. *International Journal of Educational Research, 50*(4), 251–256. doi:10.1016/j.ijer.2011.08.006

91 Steele, C., & Aronson, J. (1995). Stereotype threat and the intellectual test performance of African-Americans. *Journal of Personality and Social Psychology, 67*, 797–811.

92 Dunning, D., Heath, C., & Suls, J. M. (2004). Flawed self-assessment: Implications for health, education, and the workplace. *Psychological Science in the Public Interest, 5*(3), 69–106.

93 Brown, G. T. L., & Harris, L. R. (2014). The future of self-assessment in classroom practice: Reframing self-assessment as a core competency. *Frontline Learning Research, 3*, 22–30. doi:10.14786/flr.v2i1.24

94 Nelson, T. O., & Narens, L. (1990). Metamemory: A theoretical framework and new findings. *The Psychology of Learning and Motivation, 26*, 125–141.

95 Bourke, R. (2014). Self-assessment in professional programmes within tertiary institutions. *Teaching in Higher Education, 19*(8), 908–918. doi:10.1080/13562517.2014.934353

96 Falchikov, N., & Boud, D. (1989). Student self-assessment in higher education: A meta-analysis. *Review of Educational Research, 59*(4), 395–430.

97 Leahy, S., Lyon, C., Thompson, M., & Wiliam, D. (2005). Classroom assessment minute by minute, day by day. *Educational Leadership, 63*(3), 18–24.

98 Baars, M., Vink, S., van Gog, T., de Bruin, A., & Paas, F. (2014). Effects of training self-assessment and using assessment standards on retrospective and prospective monitoring of problem solving. *Learning and Instruction, 33*, 92–107. doi:10.1016/j.learninstruc.2014.04.004

99 Topping, K. J. (2013). Peers as a source of formative and summative assessment. In J. H. McMillan (Ed.), *The SAGE handbook of research on classroom assessment* (pp. 395–412). Thousand Oaks, CA: Sage.

100 Panadero, E. (2016). Is it safe? Social, interpersonal, and human effects of peer assessment: A review and future directions. In G. T. L. Brown, & L. R. Harris (Eds.), *Handbook of human and social conditions in assessment* (pp. 247–266). New York: Routledge.

References

101 van Gennip, N. A. E., Segers, M. S. R., & Tillema, H. H. (2010). Peer assessment as a collaborative learning activity: The role of interpersonal variables and conceptions. *Learning and Instruction*, 20(4), 280–290.

102 Strijbos, J. W. (2016). Assessment of collaborative learning. In G. T. L. Brown, & L. R. Harris (Eds.), *Handbook of human and social conditions in assessment* (pp. 302–318). New York: Routledge.

103 Lipnevich, A. A., Berg, D. A. G., & Smith, J. K. (2016). Toward a model of student response to feedback. In G. T. L. Brown, & L. R. Harris (Eds.), *The handbook of human and social conditions in assessment* (pp. 169–185). New York: Routledge.

104 Panadero, E., Romero, M., & Strijbos, J. W. (2013). The impact of a rubric and friendship on construct validity of peer assessment, perceived fairness and comfort, and performance. *Studies in Educational Evaluation*, 39(4), 195–203. doi:10.1016/j.stueduc.2013.10.005

105 Falchikov, N., & Goldfinch, J. (2000). Student peer assessment in higher education: A meta-analysis comparing peer and teacher marks. *Review of Educational Research*, 70(3), 287–322.

106 Lam, S. W. M. (2011). *Students' perceptions towards peer assessment in tertiary education in Chinese society*. (BEd (Hons) unpublished dissertation), Hong Kong Institute of Education, Hong Kong.

107 Hattie, J., & Timperley, H. (2007). The power of feedback. *Review of Educational Research*, 77(1), 81–112.

108 Sadler, D. R. (2010). Beyond feedback: Developing student capability in complex appraisal. *Assessment & Evaluation in Higher Education*, 35(5), 535–550.

109 Brown, G. T. L., Peterson, E. R., & Yao, E. S. (2016). Student conceptions of feedback: Impact on self-regulation, self-efficacy, and academic achievement. *British Journal of Educational Psychology*, 86(4), 606-629. doi:10.1111/bjep.12126

110 Kluger, A. N., & DeNisi, A. (1996). The effects of feedback interventions on performance: A historical review, a meta-analysis, and a preliminary feedback intervention theory. *Psychological Bulletin*, 119(2), 254–284.

111 Boekaerts, M., & Corno, L. (2005). Self-regulation in the classroom: A perspective on assessment and intervention. *Applied Psychology: An International Review*, 54(2), 199–231.

References

112 Harris, L. R., Brown, G. T. L., & Harnett, J. A. (2014). Understanding classroom feedback practices: A study of New Zealand student experiences, perceptions, and emotional responses. *Educational Assessment, Evaluation and Accountability*, 26(2), 107–133. doi:10.1007/s11092-013-9187-5

113 Harris, L., Brown, G., & Harnett, J. (2015). Analysis of New Zealand primary and secondary student peer- and self-assessment comments: Applying Hattie and Timperley's feedback model. *Assessment in Education: Principles, Policy & Practice*, 22(2), 265–281. doi:10.1080/0969594X.2014.976541

114 Gan, M. J. S., & Hattie, J. (2014). Prompting secondary students' use of criteria, feedback specificity and feedback levels during an investigative task. *Instructional Science*, 42(6), 861–878. doi:10.1007/s11251-014-9319-4

115 Brown, G. T. L., Harris, L. R., & Harnett, J. (2012). Teacher beliefs about feedback within an assessment for learning environment: Endorsement of improved learning over student well-being. *Teaching and Teacher Education*, 28(7), 968–978. doi:10.1016/j.tate.2012.05.003

116 Shulman, L. S. (1987). Knowledge and teaching: Foundations of the new reform. *Harvard Educational Review*, 57(1), 1–21.

117 Clarke, S., Timperley, H. S., & Hattie, J. A. (2003). *Unlocking formative assessment: Practical strategies for enhancing students' learning in the primary and intermediate classroom* (New Zealand ed.). Auckland, NZ: Hodder Moa Beckett.

118 Shute, V. J. (2008). Focus on formative feedback. *Review of Educational Research*, 78(1), 153–189.

119 Waltman, K. K., & Frisbie, D. A. (1994). Parents' understanding of their children's report card grades. *Applied Measurement in Education*, 7(3), 223–240.

120 Guskey, T. R. (1996). Reporting on student learning: Lessons from the past-prescriptions for the future. In T. R. Guskey (Ed.), *Communicating student learning* (pp. 13–24). Alexandria, VA: Association for Supervision and Curriculum Development.

121 McMillan, J. H. (2001). Secondary teachers' classroom assessment and grading practices. *Educational Measurement: Issues and Practice*, 20(1), 20–32.

References

122 Stiggins, R. J., Frisbie, D. A., & Grisworld, P. A. (1989). Inside high school grading practices: Building a research agenda. *Educational Measurement: Issues and Practice*, 8(2), 5–14.

123 Hawe, E. M. (2002). Assessment in a pre-service teacher education programme: The rhetoric and the practice of standards-based assessment. *Asia-Pacific Journal of Teacher Education*, 30(1), 93–106.

124 Muñoz, M. A., & Guskey, T. R. (2015). Standards-based grading and reporting will improve education. *Phi Delta Kappan*, 96(7), 64–68.

125 Jaeger, R. M., & Putnam, S. E. (1994). *Communicating to parents and school board members through school report cards: Effective strategies.* Paper presented at the Annual Meeting of the North Carolina Association for Research in Education, Greensboro, NC.

126 Hattie, J., & Peddie, R. (2003). School reports: 'Praising with faint damns'. *Set: Research Information for Teachers*, 3, 4–9.

127 Robinson, V., Timperley, H., Ward, L., Tuioto, L., Stevenson, V. T., & Mitchell, S. (2004). *Strengthening Education in Mangere and Otara Evaluation: Final Evaluation Report.* Auckland, NZ: Auckland UniServices Ltd.

128 Koretz, D., & Hamilton, L. (2006). Testing for accountability in K-12. In R. L. Brennan (Ed.), *Educational Measurement* (pp. 531–621). Westport, CT: Praeger.

129 Cook, T. D., & Campbell, D. T. (1979). Causal inference and the language of experimentation. In T. D. Cook, & D. T. Campbell (Eds.), *Quasi-experimentation: Design & analysis issues for field settings* (pp. 1–36). Boston, MA: Houghton Mifflin.

130 Hovland, C. I., Lumsdaine, A. A., & Sheffield, F. D. (1955). A baseline for measurement of percentage change. In P. F. Lazarsfeld, & M. Rosenberg (Eds.), *The language of social research: A reader in the methodology of social research* (pp. 77–82). New York: The Free Press.

131 Hattie, J. A., & Brown, G. T. L. (2010). Assessment and evaluation. In C. Rubie-Davies (Ed.), *Educational psychology: Concepts, research and challenges* (pp. 102–117). Abingdon, UK: Routledge.

132 Brown, G. T. L. (2016). The qualitative secret within quantitative research: It's not just about numbers. In C. J. McDermott, & Kožuh, B. (Eds.). *Modern approaches in social and educational research* (pp. 33–42). Antioch University: Los Angeles, CA.

133 Hattie, J. A. C., Brown, G. T. L., & Keegan, P. J. (2003). A national teacher-managed, curriculum-based assessment system: Assessment

Tools for Teaching & Learning (asTTle). *International Journal of Learning*, 10, 771–778.
134 Brown, G. T. L. (2004). Measuring attitude with positively packed self-report ratings: Comparison of agreement and frequency scales. *Psychological Reports*, 94(3), 1015–1024. doi:10.2466/pr0.94.3.1015-1024
135 Rodriguez, M. C. (2005). Three options are optimal for multiple-choice items: A meta-analysis of 80 years of research. *Educational Measurement: Issues and Practice*, 24(2), 3–13.
136 Kubiszyn, T., & Borich, G. D. (2012). *Educational testing and measurement: Classroom application and practice* (10th ed.). New York: John Wiley & Sons.
137 Miller, D. M., Linn, R. L., & Gronlund, N. E. (2013). *Measurement and assessment in teaching* (11th ed.). Boston, MA: Pearson.
138 Thorndike, R. M., & Thorndike-Christ, T. (2010). *Measurement and evaluation in psychology and education* (8th ed.). Boston, MA: Pearson.
139 Russell, M. K., & Airasian, P. W. (2012). *Classroom assessment: Concepts and applications* (7th ed.). New York: McGraw Hill.
140 Carlson, S. B. (1985). *Creative classroom testing: Ten designs for assessment and instruction*. Princeton, NJ: Educational Testing Service.
141 Foster, D. (2010, July). *Common sources of construct irrelevant variance and what can be done about them*. Paper presented at the biennial conference of the International Test Commission, Hong Kong.
142 Alderson, C. J. (1983). The cloze procedure and proficiency in English as a foreign language. In J. W. Oller (Ed.), *Issues in language testing research* (pp. 205–217). Rowley, MA: Newbury House Publishers.
143 Sweller, J. (2006). The worked example effect and human cognition. *Learning and Instruction*, 16(2), 165–169.
144 Kiewra, K. A., & Dubois, N. F. (1997). *Learning to learn: Making the transition from student to life-long learner*. Boston, MA: Allyn & Bacon.
145 Crocker, L. M., & Algina, J. (1986). *Introduction to classical and modern test theory*. New York: Holt, Rinehart, and Winston.
146 Hambleton, R. K., Swaminathan, H., & Rogers, H. J. (1991). *Fundamentals of item response theory*. Newbury Park, CA: Sage.
147 Dweck, C. S. (1986). Motivational processes affecting learning. *American Psychologist*, 41(10), 1040–1048.
148 Masters, G. N. (1982). A Rasch model for partial credit scoring. *Psychometrika*, 47(2), 149–174.
149 Samejima, F. (1969). Estimation of latent ability using a response pattern of graded scores. *Psychometrika Monograph Supplement*, 34(4, Pt. 2), 100.

References

150 Wainer, H., Bradlow, E. T., & Wang, X. (2007). *Testlet response theory and its applications*. Cambridge, UK: Cambridge University Press.

151 Sijtsma, K. (2009). On the use, the misuse, and the very limited usefulness of Cronbach's alpha. *Psychometrika*, 74(1), 107–120. doi:10.1007/S11336-008-9101-0

152 Harvill, L. M. (1991). Standard error of measurement. *Educational Measurement: Issues and Practice*, 10(2), 33–41. doi:10.1111/j.1745-3992.1991.tb00195.x

153 Wedman, J., & Lyrén, P.-E. (2015). Methods for examining the psychometric quality of subscores: A review and application. *Practical Assessment, Research & Evaluation*, 20(21). Retrieved from http://pareonline.net/getvn.asp?v=20&n=21.

154 Haertel, E. H. (2006). Reliability. In R. L. Brennan (Ed.), *Educational measurement* (4th ed., pp. 65–110). Westport, CT: Praeger.

155 Cronbach, L. J. (1951). Coefficient alpha and the internal structure of tests. *Psychometrika*, 16, 297–334.

156 Embretson, S. E., & Reise, S. P. (2000). *Item response theory for psychologists*. Mahwah, NJ: Lawrence Erlbaum Associates.

157 Kao, G., & Thompson, J. S. (2003). Racial and ethnic stratification in educational achievement and attainment. *Annual Review of Sociology*, 29(1), 417–442. doi:10.1146/annurev.soc.29.010202.100019

158 Sirin, S. R. (2005). Socioeconomic status and academic achievement: A meta-analytic review of research. *Review of Educational Research*, 75(3), 417–453. doi:10.3102/00346543075003417

159 Buckendahl, C. W. (2016). Public perceptions about assessment in education. In G. T. L. Brown, & L. R. Harris (Eds.), *Handbook of human and social conditions in assessment* (pp. 454–471). New York: Routledge.

160 Moon, T. R. (2016). Differentiated instruction and assessment: An approach to classroom assessment in conditions of student diversity. In G. T. L. Brown, & L. R. Harris (Eds.), *Handbook of human and social conditions in assessment* (pp. 284–301). New York: Routledge.

161 Mertler, C. A. (2002). *Using standardized test data to guide instruction and intervention*. Washington, DC: ERIC Clearinghouse on Assessment and Evaluation. (ERIC No. ED470589).

162 National Governors Association Center for Best Practices Council of Chief State School Officers. (2010). *Common core state standards*. Washington, DC: Author.

163 Glaser, R. (1963). Instructional technology and the measurement of learning outcomes: Some questions. *American Psychologist*, 18(8), 519–521. doi:10.1037/h0049294

164 Hambleton, R. K. (1994). The rise and fall of criterion-referenced measurement? *Educational Measurement: Issues and Practice*, 13(4), 21–27.

165 Cizek, G. J. (Ed.). (2001). *Setting performance standards: Concepts, methods, and perspectives.* Mahwah, NJ: Lawrence Erlbaum Associates.

166 Turner, C. E., & Upshur, J. A. (1996). Developing rating scales for the assessment of second language performance. *Australian Review of Applied Linguistics, Series S*, 13, 55–79.

167 Angoff, W. H. (1974). Criterion-referencing, norm-referencing and the SAT. *The College Board Review*, 92, 3–5, 21.

168 National Council on Measurement in Education. (2016). *Glossary of important assessment and measurement terms.* Retrieved from www.ncme.org/ncme/NCME/Resource_Center/NCME/Resource_Center/Glossary1.aspx.

Index

Note: Italicized page numbers indicate a figure on the corresponding page. Page numbers in bold indicate a table on the corresponding page.

academic performance and feedback 83
accuracy of scoring 34
adaptive conceptions of assessment 9
age equivalent scores 122
American AP Studio Art evaluation 49
analytic rubric 31–3
'approximate' basis in scoring 103
assessment-like interactions 26
assessments: assumptions of 20–6; authentic assessment 50–6; challenges of 48–50; computer assessments of essays 37; conceptions of 2, 4, 5–10; ego-protective approach to 85; essay question assessment/test 18, 42–4; formative assessment 7, 26, 27–8, 32–3; fundamental goals of 4; introduction to 1–3; as learning 16; for learning 57; overview of 3–5; standardised tests 116, 119; student involvement in assessments 57–66; summary of 10–12; summative assessment 7–8, 26–8, 32; *see also* classroom assessment; evaluations; objectively scored assessments; scores/scoring assessments; self-assessment; tests/testing
assessment theory 3
authentic assessment 50–6
Authentic Assessment Toolbox 54
autonomy of students 61

'best' answer 95
biased scoring 26
binary-choice questions 99, 99–102, *100*, *101*

chance-adjusted correlation 34
check-marking 40
child-centred concerns 84
class-generated criteria 64–5
classical test theory 113
classroom assessment: authentic assessment 50–6; error in human judgements 36–41; essays and 42–4; exemplar and 35–6; introduction to 9, 12, 29; portfolio assessment 44–50; rubrics and 29–35; small-scale marking in classrooms 39
cognitive skills and teaching 90
complex processing 15

Index

computer assessments of essays 37
computer-based testing 101
conceptions: adaptive conceptions of assessment 9; of assessments 2, 4, 5–10
Confucian approaches to learning 7
consistency of scoring 34
constructed response item formats 102–6
content knowledge of teachers 16
correlation: of agreement 43; chance-adjusted correlation 34; degrees of 113; inter-item correlations 114; inter-rater correlations 35; between markers 34; self-evaluations vs. test score ratings 60; split-half inter-item correlations 114
correlations: total score correlations 114
criterion referenced interpretation of scores 85, 117, 123–4
curriculum alignment/expectations 14–15, 18, 90

data-collection methods 18
dichotomous score calculation 110–11
differential impact 26
discrepancy in scoring 34–5
discriminations 24, 93
distractors in multiple-choice questions 92, 93
double-marking 40

educational assessment, defined 1
efficacy of students 44
ego-protective approach to assessment 85
environmental distractions 37–8
e-portfolios 44, 45–6

error in human judgement 36–41
errors in assessment process 25
essay question assessment/test 18, 42–4
evaluations: American AP Studio Art evaluation 49; by collegues/peers 58, 71; person-oriented evaluation 78; portfolio of 47; self-evaluations 59–61, 66; techniques of 76; *see also* assessments
'exact match' basis in scoring 103
exemplar in scoring 35–6
experiences with assessments 1–2
explicit criteria and standards 15–17

favouritism 41
feedback, grading, and reporting: academic performance and 83; construct being sampled 89; grading feedback 80–4; guidance for 90; introduction 73–4; lack of from teachers 57; peer feedback 57–8, 63, 76; principles of 74–80; reporting of 84–6, 90; self-focused feedback 75; self-oriented feedback 75; self-regulation in 74–6; student-student feedback 75
Feedback Intervention model 75
formative assessment 7, 26, 27–8, 32–3
fundamental goals of assessment 4

generalisability theory methods 37
grade equivalent scores 122
grading feedback 80–4; *see also* feedback, grading, and reporting
graphical representation of objects 105–6

halo effect 40
higher-order skills 15, 37, 42–3
highlighting/underlining format 103–4
holistic rubric 31–3, 68
honour code against cheating 69

improvement-oriented assessment 18–20, 20
insert missing material 102–3
inter-item correlations 114
internalisation of assessment standards 62
inter-rater correlations 35
in-the-moment evidence 26
intuitive judgements 26
ipsative-referenced interpretation 85, 86, 117
irrelevance of assessment 4
Item Response Theory (IRT) 109, 110
item writing in multiple choice questions 95

judgement of learning 66
judgement-scoring: assessment challenges 48–50; authentic assessment 50–6; differences in 37–8; error in human judgement 36–41; essay question assessment 42–4; exemplar in scoring 35–6; introduction to 25, 29; markers 39–41; portfolio assessment 44–8; rubric for 29–35, 67; task/prompt quality 38–9

key, in multiple-choice questions 92–3

learning improvements 4
Likert scale 64

low-opportunity public examination systems 7

margin of error 115
markers and rubrics 34–5, 39–41
maximum wrong discrepancy value 98
median percentile 120
memory and recall skills 15
merit grades 67
metacognitive processes 45, 47
methodological robustness 17–18
mix-and-match/lists format 95–7, 96, 97
multiple-choice questions (MCQs) 18, 87, 91–5, 94

Normal Curve Equivalent (NCE) 121
norm-referenced interpretation 85, 116, 117–22

objectively scored assessments: binary-choice questions 99, 99–102, 100, 101; constructed response item formats 102–6; graphical representation of objects 105–6; highlighting/underlining format 103–4; insert missing material 102–3; introduction 12, 87–8; measurement/recording tools 106; mix-and-match/lists format 95–7, 96, 97; multiple-choice questions 18, 87, 91–5, 94; selected response item formats 91–102; sequencing response 97–9, 98; short answer format 104–5, 105; summary of 107–8; test design 88–91, **90**
obtained/observed (O) score 113
on-the-fly evidence 26

Index

Page, Ellis 43
paper-and-pencil testing 55
partial credit modeling 111
passive voice verbs 43
pedagogical content knowledge 77
peer assessment 67–72, 75
peer evaluations 58, 71
peer feedback 57–8, 63, 76
PeerWise 69
percentile in scoring 120–1
perceptions of assessment 2
permanent exemplar 36
person-oriented evaluation 78
pointless assessment 3
poor assessment practices 10
portfolio assessment 44–8
precision of scoring 34
prepositions for assessment 26–8
principles of assessment:
   assessment assumptions
   20–6; curriculum alignment
   14–15; explicit criteria and
   standards 15–17; improvement-
   oriented assessment 18–20,
   20; introduction to 13–14;
   methodological robustness
   17–18; prepositions for
   assessment 26–8; summary
   of 28
professionalism requirements 13
progress scale 30
project learning activities 58
PROVEE.IT model 48

rank-order scores 85, 124–5
rating process 30
reliability of scores 112–16
reporting: construct being sampled
   89; of feedback 84–6, 90;
   guidance for 90; introduction
   to 11–12, 17, 22; self-reporting
   66; student mark for 63;
   teachers to parents 84, 121;
   see also feedback, grading, and
   reporting
rubrics: analytic rubric 31–3;
   holistic rubric 31–3, 68; for
   judgement-scoring 29–35, 67;
   peer assessment and 67, 71–2;
   summative assessment 32

school accountability 4, 6
scientific research in education 17
scores/scoring assessments:
   accuracy of scoring 34; age/
   grade equivalent scores 122;
   'approximate' basis 103;
   biased scoring 26; calculation
   of 109–12; consistency of
   34; criterion referenced
   interpretation 85, 117, 123–4;
   dichotomous score calculation
   110–11; discrepancy in 34–5;
   'exact match' basis 103;
   exemplar in 35–6; interpretation
   of 116–25; introduction to 109;
   Normal Curve Equivalent 121;
   norm-referenced interpretation
   85, 116, 117–22; percentile
   in 120–1; precision of 34;
   rank-order scores 85, 124–5;
   rating calculations 111–12;
   reliability of 112–16; standard
   error of measurement 110, 112,
   115–16; standard/scale scores
   122; stanine score 121; student
   scoring differences 37–8; *see also*
   judgement-scoring; objectively
   scored assessments
seat-work assessments 53
selected response item formats
   91–102

Index

self-assessment: class-generated criteria 64–5; examples of 64–6; judgement of learning 66; overview of 59–62; self-marking 63–4; self-rating inventory 64; traffic lights assessment 65–6
self-evaluations 59–61, 66
self-focused feedback 75
self-marking 63–4
self-oriented feedback 75
self-rating inventory 64
self-regulation of learning 59, 69, 74–6
self-reporting 66
sequencing response 97–9, 98
short answer format 91, 104–5, 105
small-scale marking in classrooms 39
social consequences 13
social groups 7
split-half inter-item correlations 114
standard deviations 110
standard error of measurement (SEM) 110, 112, 115–16
standardised tests 112, 116, 119
standards-based curricula 83
standard/scale scores 122
stanine score 121
statistics *see* scores/scoring assessments
stem in multiple-choice questions, the 92
Student Conceptions of Assessment inventory 10
student involvement in assessments 57–66
students: achievement/learning of 4, 6; autonomy of 61; conceptions of assessment 8–10; efficacy of 44; performance contributors 13–14; scoring differences 37–8; self-evaluations 60–1; task/prompt quality 38–9; testing as motivation 19
student-student feedback 75
summative assessment 7–8, 26–8, 32

task/prompt quality 38–9
teachers/teaching: cognitive skills and 90; content knowledge of 16; decision-making of 1; improved testing outcomes 4, 19, 26; lack of feedback from 57; peer assessment and 67–72, 75; reporting to parents 84; self-evaluations 60–1; *see also* judgement-scoring
technology-based exemplar 36
technology-enhanced assessment practices 55
tests/testing: classical test theory 113; computer-based testing 101; design of 88–91, **90**; difficulty with 124; essay question assessment/test 18, 42–4; improved outcomes in 4, 19, 26; as motivation 19; paper-and-pencil testing 55; short answer format 91, 104–5, 105; standardised tests 112, 116, 119; statistics on 110; *see also* assessments
test-wise advice 89
timing importance in assessment 3
top-of-the-scale exemplar 35–6
total score correlations 114
traffic lights assessment 65–6

value-added measures in achievement 86

weighted judgement by assessor 31

For Product Safety Concerns and Information please contact our EU representative GPSR@taylorandfrancis.com
Taylor & Francis Verlag GmbH, Kaufingerstraße 24, 80331 München, Germany

www.ingramcontent.com/pod-product-compliance
Lightning Source LLC
Chambersburg PA
CBHW050538300426
44113CB00012B/2172